The US carrier
Yorktown provided
one of the great
dramas of Midway.
Here the ship's
resilience in the face
of damage at Coral
Sea, air strikes at
Midway and
eventually submarine
torpedoes is finally
overcome as she
starts to sink at dawn
on 7 June.

BATTLES IN FOCUS

MIDWAY

PHILIP D. GROVE

BRASSEY'S

First published in 2004 by Brassey's

An imprint of Chrysalis Books Group

Brassey's
The Chrysalis Building, Bramley Road,
London W10 6SP

North American orders:
Casemate Publishing, 2114 Darby Road,
Havertown, PA 19083, USA

Philip D. Grove has asserted his moral right
to be identified as the author of this work.

Library of Congress Cataloging in Publication Data
available

British Library cataloguing in Publication Data
A catalogue record for this book is available
from the British Library

ISBN 1 85753 338 0

Photograph acknowledgements: Chrysalis Images,
US Department of Defense, US Navy, US National
Archives and PageantPix.

Edited and designed by DAG Publications Ltd
Designed by David Gibbons
Edited by Roger Chesneau
Cartography and layout by Anthony A. Evans

Printed in Singapore.

CONTENTS

Preface

There are many reasons why another book dealing with Midway ought to have been written, and this is perhaps why I was lucky enough to have been given the chance to write it by Brassey's. My own interest in Midway – both personal and professional – is considerable. I have long had an interest in Japanese naval aviation, in naval aviation in general and in the Pacific War, not to mention a rather peculiar interest in counterfactual history. Professionally, this is a result of having given a forty-five minute lecture on the Battle of Midway to every young officer in the Royal Navy since 1993. However, until now, I have never had enough time to undertake what I consider sufficient research for that lecture. I therefore hope that this book will rectify matters, for myself and for my students, past, present and future. Not that I believe all of my students will immediately rush out and buy this book (although I think that they *should*!), but at least they will now have the opportunity to explore the battle, and my thoughts, at their leisure – and much more deeply than hitherto. More importantly, a far wider audience will be able to journey into one of the most crucial and decisive battles in the greatest war of the twentieth century, by means of a twenty-first century book.

As with all authors and their books, I have a large number of individuals to thank, particularly John Lee at Chrysalis, for being so patient with my deadlines, and Rod Dymott (now of Brassey's Inc.), for pandering to my interest in counter-factual history and allowing elements of it into the following pages – and, of course, for encouraging me to write them in the first place; my Department of Strategic Studies and the Library in Britannia Royal Naval College, for things far too many to mention; and my parents for 'establishing' me in the first place. I thank also, of course, my wife Rachel, for putting up with me during the time spent writing, attending conferences and seminars and tackling College work (and during the occasional grumps), and for her great skill and patience in helping me piece the jigsaw together. All I can say is, 'hurrah and hurrumph'; she will know what I mean! All this said, if there are factual errors to be found, then, as all authors ought to say (and most actually do), 'I and I alone am responsible for them.'

Introduction

Without doubt, the Battle of Midway is one of the most famous naval encounters in history. It is also one of the few *decisive* battles in the chronicles of naval warfare. It is also a rarity in that it took place against a backdrop of massive changes in naval technologies and tactics – most importantly, the maturing technology of aircraft and the impact of carrier air power on naval warfare. It was not the first battle in which fleets fought each other without sighting the enemy – that was Coral Sea, in May 1942 – but it was the first decisive battle that saw not ships but naval aircraft as the decisive element in the confrontation. The aircraft carrier and its embarked air group was a weapons system that was barely twenty-five years old, originating when the First World War gave birth to naval aviation. Midway was decisive because it witnessed a clash of two fleets in the centre of the Pacific in June 1942 the outcome of which was to change not merely the course of the Pacific War, but also technology, naval warfare in general and, politically, both America and the Pacific Ocean.

Much has been written about the battle. Since the end of World War II, histories both detailed and brief, 'coffee table' books and novels have all been published by the dozen, each revisiting the death throes of the Japanese carriers, the valiant yet fruitless US torpedo-bomber attacks and the successful exploits of US dive-bombers. Perhaps just as much attention to the subject has been paid by producers of Hollywood films and of television documentaries around the world. Even though we have John Ford's first-hand footage of the attack on Midway and, from the 1960s, Charlton Heston's aerial bravery in the film *Battle of Midway*, do we really understand the real story? How has the interpretation of time, and the passing of more than 60 years, affected the telling and understanding of one of the greatest sea battles in history? This battle was, potentially, a 'decider' concerning the American way of life during the dark, desperate days in the summer of 1942, and consequently a 'decider' concerning the fate of the rest of the world.

In order, it is hoped, to demonstrate that the full story of Midway has yet to be told, this book takes the reader through familiar ground but also poses, and answers, a number of not-so-familiar questions. Some of the topics raised have been tackled in previous texts, but never before, I suggest, together in a compact volume such as the present work.

The importance of the battle to the course of the Pacific War, and its place in wider history, are both immense and (supposedly) very well known. Consequently, accounts of Midway tend to suffer from a degree of familiarity and tiredness. These are both very dangerous attitudes in history's pursuit of understanding events and the search for the truth: myths and misconceptions are born, rapidly replacing the facts. Midway – indeed, the Pacific War as a whole –

is no stranger to these trends. For example, among the popular beliefs is one that Yamamoto was a great Admiral, and was America's greatest foe in the Pacific; another is that Nagumo was timid, generally speaking not the most intelligent Admiral, and definitely not a carrier fleet commander. It is often said that the Japanese were unfortunate and the Americans very lucky at Midway, and that the Americans were vastly outnumbered. And so forth. These and other 'truths' are some of the foremost misconceptions about the battle, and this book will seek to address them.

The traditional viewpoint of the Battle of Midway in June 1942 is that, 'completely outnumbered and due to be overwhelmed by the unstoppable Japanese juggernaut, Admiral Nimitz dispatched his last three Pacific carriers to stop the Japanese invasion of Midway. Were Midway to fall then the whole of the American western seaboard was open to Japanese attack. On June 4th, 1942 as the Japanese and US forces approached the island of Midway, they encountered each other. In the ensuing battle the Americans saw their carrier *Yorktown* sink in exchange for four of the Japanese carriers and their air crews – the heart of their carrier striking power – forcing Admiral Yamamoto to return to Japan. From that point on, the Japanese offensive had been checked, and it was only a matter of time before American victory.' There is much to say for this viewpoint, but there are also far too many simplifications and generalisations for it to ring completely true to the twenty-first century reader and researcher.

In the following chapters the reader will be introduced to the background of the Pacific War and the encounter at Midway in particular. The Japanese plan of attack and the American defensive measures will then be analysed, and then the key players involved in the battle will be assessed, together with the aircraft and ships of the two opposing forces. The battle will then be discussed before a final analysis is offered – the impact of the battle and its place in the Pacific War – and conclusions are drawn. It is hoped that the reader will then be convinced that the Battle of Midway was far from a battle of effective planning, good luck and great bravery. In fact, it was a battle decided as a result of a myriad of contributory factors, some of which have either been overlooked or simply not given the same significance and importance as other, seemingly more memorable events or circumstances. Some, it would appear, have been underplayed, either accidentally or deliberately, in order to give an oft-recounted tale that is far from being a full account of the battle, the people involved and the outcome.

It is undeniable that the Battle of Midway marked the beginning of the turning point in the Pacific War. The Japanese onslaught, spearheaded by its carrier force and her naval aviators, was irrevocably stopped. Japanese losses at Midway were not just material, involving her four carriers and some 270 carrier-based aircraft, but also human. The loss of some of the Imperial Japanese Navy's best air crews and many of its experienced and capable ground crews was perhaps the biggest blow. Most of them were of the highest calibre, not just amongst their peers back in Japan but amongst the world's naval and perhaps even non-naval fields. Years of training and combat experience vanished for want of a few handfuls of bombs, a warriors' code, and ship survivability.

The losses were much more important than simple numbers of ships and aircraft. The *matériel* could be replaced in months, but not air crews or support staff – certainly not personnel with sufficient training and experience. When Japan entered the war with America in December 1941, she did so with a thousand highly trained aviators flying a thousand high-quality aircraft, supported by just a few thousand highly skilled and professional maintenance personnel on board more aircraft carriers than the United States Navy possessed. After Midway, this superiority would never be regained.

What is often forgotten is the fact that, at Midway, losses amongst the Imperial Japanese Navy flyers were in fact far fewer than might normally have been accepted: more than half of the Japanese aviators involved survived the battle. Unfortunately, it was the IJN's experienced mechanics and support crews who did not live to fight on. In excess of 2,000 of these support personnel, aircraft maintenance staff and engineers perished with the four Japanese carriers, and it was these losses, in an already overstretched navy, that were difficult to replace. They have to be taken in conjunction with Japan's mounting losses during the earlier Indian Ocean incursion by Admiral Nagumo in April 1942 and the IJN's casualties incurred during the Battle of the Coral Sea in May 1942. By the end of the Battle of Midway, the heart of Japan's most potent striking force had been mortally wounded: Japan would never again group together so many able flyers in aircraft that were superior to America's, maintained by extremely proficient support staff, as she had for the first six months of the Pacific War. Essentially, Midway was responsible for forcing Japan on to the strategic defensive in the Pacific, whilst simultaneously quickening the pace of American victory. By the summer of 1942 and Midway, the US Navy was in the throes of a massive air crew and engineer training drive that would pay dividends into 1943.

Yet Midway was a battle that should have seen America doomed to lose: supposedly, Japan's overwhelming strength and superiority, and her previous successes, should have conspired to see the IJN victorious again. Her defensive perimeter had by this time been extended and US Pacific influence shattered, completing the task begun on 7 December 1941 when Japanese Admiral Nagumo had attacked Pearl Harbor. The story of Midway and the reasons for the defeat of the Imperial Japanese Navy should be known by all who have an interest in naval warfare, the Pacific War and leadership.

1

BACKGROUND

THE CLASH OF HISTORY, CULTURE AND DESTINY: EVENTS PRECEDING THE BATTLE

It would be easy to ascribe the defeat of the Japanese at Midway to a combination of simple, 'popular' factors such as 'victory disease', an overextension of capability and a huge failure of military intelligence, as have many writers. Even Japanese authors have suggested that the incredible victories in the early months of the war clouded their judgement and perception of the Americans in June 1942, but is it really that simple? In all certainty, no. There were many reasons for the American victory at Midway, and in order to understand them it is necessary to look back to the time before the Pacific War – before, even, the beginning of the twentieth century.

The Japan of today is very much a creation of the years following 1853, when the country was first opened up to the modern world by Commodore Perry of the US Navy and his flotilla of four warships. Soon after this momentous event, Japan embraced the communications, technologies and military thinking of the Western world. From a naval point of view, she was quick to adopt Britain, and the Royal Navy specifically, as her role model in all naval matters. Training, ships, equipment and even ethos were garnered from the British, and the result was an increasingly powerful navy, and British input combined with Japanese direction and innovation saw imperial ambitions harboured and soon achieved. Wars with China (1894) and Russia (1904–05) resulted in victories for the Imperial Japanese Navy and a formal alliance from 1902 with the British. In World War I, naval action in support of Japanese foreign policy towards the Asian mainland and the Anglo-Japanese alliance helped the Japanese Navy – and the country as a whole – to prosper and grow. Indeed, by the end of the Great War, numerically and technologically Japan stood third in the naval rankings of the world. She wished to improve this position further. Her empire on the Asian mainland had grown, and, following the Treaty of Versailles in 1919, she was also in possession of former German Pacific territories, extending her influence even further from her shores.

However, the inter-war years were often a time of confusion and contradiction, not least for the Japanese Navy, which was grappling with the new technologies and doctrine that all major navies were struggling to come to terms with. There were also wider issues concerning her strategic security. Her alliance with the British ended in 1922 when the Washington Naval Treaty was signed, and her growing imperial ambitions likewise ended, at least for the 1920s, at that conference. Resentment grew towards the United States, which seemed intent on limiting Japan to the position of an inferior. This seemed apparent in both geographical and military terms as the Washington Naval Conference limited all the major powers and their fleets, but the Japanese believed that they had suffered most at the hands of this US brokered conference.

The Japanese government and even elements within the Imperial Japanese Navy were generally content to accept the decisions made in Washington. For the government, this was partly for economic reasons. The IJN, on the other hand, wished to take stock of the lessons of World War I. A period of stability was required in order to address the new technologies of the day, particularly with regard to aircraft and submarines, and by the mid 1920s a number of junior naval officers were already suggesting that the old technologies, doctrines and tactics were outdated and that evolution was required. This was a call echoed in most navies, but the IJN seemed more willing to accommodate these calls – or, at the very least, listen to them – than its American and European counterparts. All the time, however, the Japanese Navy was functioning in a country that was moving ever closer to national militaristic domination and ever further from Western democratic ideals. By the beginning of the 1930s, Japan had become quite fixed in her direction: nationalistic, expansionist forces would push for further incursion into mainland China, and eventual conflict with America (and possibly even Britain) in South-East Asia was countenanced to achieve these objectives.

The Washington Naval Conference, which took place from November 1921 until February 1922, was convened for a number of reasons. Public fears over an arms race between the major naval powers, combined with tensions concerning the future of China combining with private American naval desires to equal the size and strength of the Royal Navy whilst simultaneously undermining the Anglo-Japanese Naval Alliance all came together to see the great powers agree to the Washington Conference. It resulted in not one but three treaties, signed by the naval powers present.

The Four-Power Treaty was signed by the United States, Great Britain, Japan and France and effectively replaced the Anglo-Japanese Alliance of 1902. This alliance was due for renewal in 1922, and there were many in the United States, and some in the British Government and Empire, who wished to see it expire, although the Japanese Navy and large elements within Britain and the Empire wanted it to remain in force. A compromise agreement, far looser than the 1902 treaty, was therefore drafted. Its one major concession to Japan was that it forbade any navy from building an offensive naval base within 1,000 miles of Japanese waters.

The Five-Power Treaty dealt with warship size and numbers, and is discussed in further detail below. One interesting point is that it was the world's first disarmament treaty. Significantly, it actually did lead to disarmament, encompassing a reduction in warship numbers. It is generally regarded as the most important of the inter-war naval treaties.

The Nine-Power Treaty was signed in an attempt to stop any excessive exploitation of China by foreign powers. It was signed by all interested parties and remained in force during the 1920s.

By the end of World War I, however, the United States had sunk back into a foreign policy of isolation: neither the American public nor their politicians wanted any more dealings with the old countries of Europe, or even of the wider world. There were, however, a number of exceptions. One area of note was the Pacific, and especially China. The other policy aim was the avoidance of war and,

The major treaty resulting from the **Washington Naval Conference** is often referred to as the 'Five Power Treaty'. The naval powers ratifying it were the United States, Great Britain, Japan, France and Italy. This Treaty was concerned primarily with battleships. The battleship was seen, as it had been seen before World War I, as a badge of rank. Tensions continued to exist between the victorious powers after the Great War, and these were being turned into physical form in a new arms race involving new battleships and battlecruisers. The Five Power Treaty was designed to end this race, introducing a ratio that would see a downsizing of the great fleets and a series of constraints affecting individual ship displacements and gun calibres.

In terms of total naval tonnages, the ratio introduced for the five signatories was (in the order given above) 5:5:3:1.75:1.75, although in practice the French and Italian figures were treated as 2 rather than 1.75. France and Italy were not too concerned about their small allowance, just so long as neither navy was larger than the other: they were involved in their own arms race. The German Navy had been dealt with in the Treaty of Versailles. The once great German Navy had been effectively limited to a coastal force with a handful of pre-dreadnought battleships with limited firepower and a small number of cruisers. Additionally, the navy was denied submarines and an air arm. Whilst Imperial Russia (now the Soviet Union) had imploded into civil war and remained outside the mainstream of international politics. What this meant in practical terms was vastly reduced numbers of capital ships by the end of the 1920s as the Treaty began to come into force. The five navies were allowed to possess individual battleships and battlecruisers in the same ratio: 15 for the US and Royal Navies, 9 for the IJN and 6 each for the French and Italian Navies.

as a corollary, the limiting of defence spending. The Washington Naval Treaty was America's first and most important attempt to achieve these aims. The results for the US and her Navy were, on the whole, very successful. The outcome and the various treaties signed after the Conference ended any immediate cause for war, settled the limits of exploitation on the Asian mainland, particularly by Japan, and replaced the Anglo-Japanese Alliance with something far less tangible and much less exclusive. It capped Japan's strength and that of the Royal Navy, whilst leaving the strength of the US Navy equal (on paper) to that of the Royal Navy and, in theory, far larger than Japan's – and with more modern ships. The American negotiators at the Conference succeeded in all of their ambitions, both the publicly articulated aims of peace and stability and the not-so-public aims of isolating Japan and achieving equality with the Royal Navy.

The Treaty acts as a useful yardstick when assessing Japan's relationship with the West in the two decades following World War I. Although all sides broke the component treaties before they expired in the 1930s, none completely undermined them during the 1920s and all the signatories were initially well-disposed towards them. Moreover, a number of conferences were convened after Washington, particularly the London Naval Conferences, which attempted to build upon the agreements reached there, although, with hindsight, these can also be seen as contributory causes of the Pacific War. The Japanese, particularly, considered the outcomes to be biased against them, complaining that disproportionate restrictions had been placed upon them and their navy. The Japanese Army, and nationalist elements in Japan, were none too pleased by what they saw as continual systematic treaties that attempted to limit their future and considerable weakness on the part of the IJN for agreeing to the limitations in the first place.

Nonetheless, the 1920s was a decade for taking stock and rebuilding, and consequently it was a decade of arms conferences, international peace treaties and the new international organisation, the League of Nations, all of which combined to place limitations upon the navies of the world. The 1930s, on the other hand, was a very different decade. Following ten years of international constraints and weak politicians, Japanese militarists and nationalists were very keen to see the humiliations of the 1920s overturned and their country's imperial policy placed firmly back on track. China was the centre of their ambitions, as it had been in the years before and during World War I. That country possessed the markets and resources needed by Japan to modernise and expand, not to mention vast tracts of land. Yet it was ruled by corruption and incompetence and split by struggle, notably between Chiang Kai-shek, the leader of the Nationalist government, and Mao Tse-tung and his communist followers. To the Japanese army on the Asian mainland, it seemed an easy target.

The Washington Treaty also addressed the question of **aircraft carriers**, although only one country, Great Britain, possessed operational warships of this kind in 1921–22. It would seem that the delegates to the conference had an inkling of the potential power of aircraft carriers: they were treated in the same ratio, and also had restrictions on displacement (between 10,000 and 27,000 tons), though not on the number of aircraft they could carry. Carriers were also defined for the first time, as ships whose primary purpose was the transportation, launching and recovery of aircraft. The maximum aggregate displacements permissible were 135,000 tons for the US and Royal Navies, 81,000 for the IJN and 60,000 tons each for the French and Italian Navies.

Without the full support of the Japanese government, Chinese Manchuria was annexed in 1931 by the Kwantung Army. This highly political and very nationalistic force was engaged in policing the Japanese-controlled railway in Manchuria, staged an excuse for action and quite quickly overcame the large but motley collection of Chinese troops and local warlords. By 1932 the Kwantung army had established the puppet state of Manchuko. In the same year, the Japanese annexed the neighbouring province of Jehol, and by 1935 Chahar province had been acquired as well. Meanwhile, in 1933, Japan left the League of Nations following criticism of her actions. The successes of the Japanese Army and the seeming lack of control displayed by Japan's government over the Kwantung Army's actions on the Asian mainland simply fuelled the thirst for expansion.

By 1937 the government of Japan was firmly under the influence and control of the militarists and nationalists, who sought further expansion. Attempts by ministers to stop aggressive actions were either ignored by the Army or resulted in their removal from office, or, worse, death by assassination. No one should stand in the way of 'Japan's destiny'. On 7 July 1937, following months of border incidents between Japanese and Nationalist Chinese troops, hostilities finally broke out between the two nations. The conflict would last eight years, spread to include the United States and Great Britain, and ultimately spell defeat for the Empire of Japan.

By August 1937 Japanese forces were successfully driving against the Chinese armies. These forces included large naval contingents, equipped with aircraft carriers and amphibious craft. The coast of China was attacked, and naval units would also be used further inland, where both troops and aircraft were used to support the army's goal of conquest. Vital combat experience for naval personnel and the designers of Japan's military equipment was being gained as a result, and much of this experience would be used to good effect by the IJN in the Pacific in December 1941.

America's initial response of caution and isolation soon became one of active, albeit low-key help towards the Chinese Nationalists. Chang Kai-shek's increasingly desperate situation, together with Japan's attacks against Western interests – and in particular the USS *Panay* incident, when an American gunboat was sunk by IJN aircraft – forced the US government to start supplying aid and, later, equipment and volunteers to the Chinese cause. In 1938, however, all President Roosevelt was able to do was to announce a 'moral embargo' against trade with Japan. Support and equipment also came to the Chinese from the Soviet Union, which only added to Japan's desire to force territorial concessions from her northern neighbour. Japanese coercion against the Soviet border regions failed, for, in the last of the ensuing military campaigns launched against Soviet forces in Mongolia in July 1939, the Kwantung Army was heavily mauled, forcing a cease-fire and eventually leading in April 1941 to a non-aggression pact between the two powers.

It became increasingly obvious to the Japanese Army that, in order to defeat Chang Kai-shek and his allies, Japan would have to cut Chinese supply lines from the outside world and, more importantly, find more sources of supply for herself. Ironically, the very reasons that found Japan fighting for territorial conquest on the Asian mainland were now driving her to consider military action further afield, in particular to the south, in the oil- and rubber-rich regions of South-East Asia. This was a course of action that was not initially favoured by the Army, but the Navy viewed these regions as not only more vulnerable but also more fulfilling from a naval operational point of view. In China, the Navy was the 'support act' for the Army, its direction and operations a result of Army planning and strategy – or so the traditional view has portrayed. A drive to the south, into South-East Asia, would, in theory at least, see the Japanese Navy become the master of its own fate; but it would also be the cause of America's entry into World War II. A number of naval officers and government ministers recognised that a southern push would definitely bring benefits, but simultaneously provide a *casus belli* for the US. Nevertheless, avoidance of war with the United States was not their major concern; rather was it the avoidance of defeat at the hands of the Americans.

In the summer of 1939, there seemed no easy way into the resource-rich southern areas. The British, French and Dutch Empires, not to mention the United States, all stood in Japan's way with an overwhelming preponderance of naval and air power. This all changed with war in Europe, and Germany's quick conquests of Poland and Western Europe. The global situation was changing drastically, and Japan was now, effectively, given a free hand in Asia. She no longer feared a war on many fronts were she to expand south: the European imperial powers had either been conquered by Hitler's Wehrmacht (France, the Netherlands, etc.) or effectively neutralised (like Britain). None of the European powers was in a position to defend its Asian colonies successfully. America posed the biggest challenge, but the Japanese military leadership correctly recognised that, in 1940, the strength of the United States lay in her navy and not in her land and air forces. America's desire for retrenchment in the inter-war years had seen the Navy funded as the defensive barrier for the continental USA, but well within the limitations of the Washington Treaty. The Army, in the meantime, lacked sufficient personnel and equipment, particularly aircraft and armoured vehicles. British-led rearmament would drastically alter this position, but in 1940 it was America rather than Japan that was a paper tiger.

The Japanese naval leadership was to the forefront in recognising the relative strengths and weaknesses of the potential protagonists. Admiral Yamamoto, the commander of the Imperial Japanese Navy's Combined Fleet (the IJN's battle-ships and aircraft carriers), and some of his fellow officers had first-hand experience of America and its military. They knew the immediate and long-term strengths of their adversary, and, in the short term, the Japanese had the upper hand. The result was a successful attempt to convince the Army of the worthiness of the mission south and, after some initial doubt and a reaffirmation of its policy towards China, the Army was won over to the Navy's way of thinking. To the Army, the move south was seen as a supporting arm of the 'China first' policy, but soon it developed a momentum all of its own. It was going to act as a springboard for future conquest into the rich colonies of South-East Asia.

In 1940, basing rights were asked of the French colonial authorities in the northern part of French Indo-China. France had been defeated by Germany, and the new Vichy regime in France, let alone the one in Indo-China, was unable to resist Japan's demands for access to bases, nor her demand to close ports to Chinese supplies. Following Japanese pressure, Britain was also forced to halt the passage of aid and equipment from Burma to the Chinese Nationalist forces. America reacted with condemnation – and further aid to China – and President Roosevelt initiated the first of his 'real' embargoes against Japanese trade. As a result, the expansion of the 'China incident', as the Japanese referred to the war against China, to include South-East Asia was now guaranteed. However, attempts at embargo and national humiliation pushed the Japanese inexorably

Japanese strategy: Japanese generals and admirals, particularly some of the latter, probably understood the latent power of the United States, and of Britain and her Empire. The IJN realised that attacking south and seizing European colonial territories would almost certainly result in the United States becoming involved in hostilities, though there was, admittedly, no absolute guarantee. Army chiefs wanted the East Indies and possibly British Malaya only, and so avoiding a conflict with the US was uppermost in their minds. However, what benefit and glory was there in this course of action for the IJN? Neither the British nor the Dutch posed a significant threat to the Japanese Navy. From the purely bureaucratic point of view of the survival and expansion of the IJN, the movement south had to be as large and as encompassing as possible. The US Navy had to be taken into account, otherwise the IJN would remain the support tool of the Japanese Army, with little rationale for its expanding carrier and battleship fleet. The Navy recognised that America in 1940 was still very much an isolationist nation, prepared to let others do the fighting ultimately beneficial to it. The US therefore had to be provoked and neutralised in the same blow – which was by no means an easy task. Curiously, if the Japanese Army had understood its naval counterpart a little better, it might have realised this and stifled the wider plan of conquest. This provides observers with a very large question. What would Roosevelt have done had American territory and possessions not been attacked in December 1941?

to war. Japan could not survive without US trade, nor could she back down in the face of US pressure. To compound the issue, Roosevelt speeded up a huge rearmament programme, augmenting it with the commencement of the draft. The US Navy benefited hugely: from June 1940, Roosevelt authorised millions of tons of new warship construction and tens of thousands of naval aircraft in an ever-expanding US Navy. The resulting fleet would ultimately become too strong for Japanese forces and ambitions, a factor well understood by the IJN's commander-in-chief, Admiral Yamamoto.

Japan's bases in northern Indo-China soon became centres of occupation, and by 24 July 1941 her forces had begun occupying the southern half of Indo-China as well. The US responded by strengthening her embargoes against Japan and by freezing Japanese assets. Britain and the Netherlands followed suit. Additionally, the US Pacific Fleet continued its process of relocation from the West Coast of America to the Hawaiian Islands, a thousand miles closer to Japan. This was intended as a physical and psychological demonstration of US intent, but it only furthered the IJN's belief in the necessity of tackling the US Navy.

Everything now hinged on the remaining months of 1941. Japan would be industrially starved by the powers that 'surrounded her', or so the militarists believed. This was an opinion shared by others, including the less militant Japanese. To avoid this dire fate, Japan would have to remove her forces from not only Indo-China but mainland China as well, and the very situation that Japanese policies had been striving for a decade to achieve – self-sufficiency within Asia – would be at an end. Perhaps worse, however, would be the national humiliation of withdrawal, and the reasons behind that withdrawal. It would not be because of an opponent's martial spirit and quality in battle (which Japanese arms were supposed to overcome), but brought about at the hands of American business power. What national honour could that hold for the Japanese people, Navy and empire? It was a fate that few in the Japanese leadership could accept. Whether or not American decision-makers were aware of this when their embargoes were put into effect is hard to know, but, either way, the normally divided Japanese military leadership of the Army and Navy now became united in their belief in a drive south, and planning for the operations to seize the territories of Malaya, Singapore and the Dutch East Indies commenced. The US-controlled Philippines was listed as well. Moreover, these islands would act as a base from which the US could attack the flanks of the Japanese onslaught into South East Asia. The IJN was now totally convinced that the US government would not stand idly by and see further Japanese conquest in Asia without taking action. However, neutralising the Americans' ability to intervene could only mean neutralising the US Pacific Fleet. The IJN would therefore have its decisive engagement, and win honour and glory.

Japan had previously initiated war against others – China in 1894 and Russia in 1904 – by means of surprise attacks, and this again seemed to be the most appropriate course of action. The Japanese naval leadership, particularly Yamamoto with his knowledge of America's latent industrial power, readily understood that any drawn-out campaign would see Japanese quality in machine and man crushed by sheer US mass production and quantity. Consequently, the only way to give Japan a fighting chance and the breathing space to employ the resources of the newly occupied areas to her advantage was a surprise, knock-out blow against the Pacific Fleet. The chances of this taking place, and of succeeding, had been increased dramatically over the previous twelve months. The redeployment of the US Pacific Fleet to Pearl Harbor in the Hawaiian Islands had brought the enemy closer. This act, seen by the US government as a step towards deterring the Japanese, actually enabled Yamamoto to countenance the belief that the IJN could destroy the US Navy in the Pacific. American action had helped bring their fleet within much closer range of Yamamoto's beloved aircraft carriers. There was now a chance of success for a surprise strike.

Additional encouragement for the attack on Hawaii came from a British strike against the Italian fleet in November 1940, when, under cover of darkness, a lone British carrier, HMS *Illustrious*, approached the Italian fleet anchorage of Taranto. The carrier then launched just 21 vulnerable, biplane Swordfish torpedo-bombers. For the loss of only two aircraft, the British disabled three Italian battleships and other targets around Taranto harbour, putting out of action half the Italian battle fleet. All of this had been achieved under the eyes of the Italians, in a shallow harbour normally precluding the use of torpedoes, and with the odds very much stacked against the British. What results, mused Yamamoto and his naval flyers, could be achieved with six larger, better-equipped carriers flying off hundreds of aircraft? Surely, they would be devastating?

USS *Shaw* exploding during the Japanese raid on Pearl Harbor, 7 December 1941. The attack on Pearl Harbor was one of the most daring raids of all time. It threw the world into total, global war and finally dragged America into armed combat. Unfortunately, it caught the United States unawares and, initially, ill-prepared for the forthcoming struggle.

Thus, in the summer of 1941, the IJN, driven by Admiral Yamamoto, on the back of its own expertise and knowledge, and buoyed by the British success, began planning and training for the drive south. This drive became an attack not merely against Western colonies and other targets in South-East Asia, but also against islands in the Pacific, territories in the Indian Ocean and Hawaii – and against the US Pacific Fleet in Pearl Harbor. The plan and its subsequent activities saw Yamamoto's Combined Fleet launch the biggest offensive in the history of warfare, with an opening front some 6,000 miles long. At the heart of this would be the Japanese carriers and land-based naval aircraft, together numbering 1,000 machines. The aim was quite simple – the total destruction of all opposing naval and air units in the Pacific. From here, Japanese Navy and Army units would engage and defeat the unprotected and unsupported land forces of America, the British Empire and the Netherlands. A defensive perimeter of island bases – 'fixed' aircraft carriers, as it were – would be established, protecting the newly won territories and providing the first line of defence. The IJN, with its battleships and carriers intact, victorious, and now dwarfing any competitor, would then act as a 'fire fighting' force, plugging any gaps in the defensive perimeter that might appear. Within this perimeter, work would be in hand to harness the resources that Japan needed to maintain her superiority over the defeated nations, and finally to come to terms with China.

The onslaught against South-East Asia and Pearl Harbor on 7 December 1941 heralded nearly six months of record-breaking offensives and victories for the Japanese and crushing defeats for the Western powers. With forces that were either numerically smaller or of similar size as those of their opponents, the Japanese swept away all-comers from South-East Asia. Surprise at Hawaii was complete, and saw the bulk of the US Pacific Fleet reduced, seemingly, to scrap metal. To compound the damage, hundreds of US aircraft were destroyed or otherwise put out of action. However, the US Pacific carriers, submarines and vital oil reserves remained intact, and would soon provide America with the ability to strike back.

However, in December 1941 the Japanese juggernaut seemed unstoppable. Amphibious landings in Malaya were under way at the time of the attack against Hawaii, and three days later the backbone of British naval power in Asia, HMS *Prince of Wales* (Prime Minister Churchill's favourite ship) and her consort, the battlecruiser HMS *Repulse*, were sunk by land-based IJN aircraft off the coast of Malaya. In quick succession, territory after territory in South-East Asia was invaded, following the Japanese plan of annihilating Allied sea and air power. By the spring of 1942, the bulk of Japan's ambitions had been met, although her great successes should have been seen in a different light – one of lost opportunities and missed chances. In early April, the bulk of the carrier forces, the First Air Fleet (or First Carrier Striking Force) that had attacked Pearl Harbor, had moved into the Indian Ocean, but, rather than push through their numerical advantage, the ships failed to destroy the newly arrived British Fleet or facilitate the seizure of any territory. The operation was simply a massed hit-and-run raid, and one that would be costly in the long term. HMS *Hermes* was sunk by IJN dive-bombers, giving Japanese carriers the distinction of achieving the first sinking in history of an aircraft carrier purely by means of aircraft flown off from the same type of ship. However, because of losses and exhaustion amongst air crews, the Japanese Navy accomplished nothing of value for future engagements, apart from a degree of over-confidence.

In April 1942, the IJN in the Indian Ocean was far superior to the Royal Navy fleet that had arrived under the command of Admiral Somerville. Somerville had

The strike against **Pearl Harbor** could have had a number of outcomes for Japan. It was very much a gamble – albeit a calculated one – by Yamamoto. Leaving aside the fact that the carriers of the US Pacific Fleet were missing and therefore escaped destruction, the chances of success for the Japanese in the Pacific War would have been far greater had Admiral Nagumo launched another wave of aircraft to strike at the port facilities and oil storage areas at Pearl Harbor. The loss of these would have greatly impaired the US Navy's ability to act, pushing it back to the West Coast of the United States, increasing transit times to theatre, denying the Americans a forward operating base at Hawaii, precluding any 'immediate' support for Midway and further isolated Australia, and thereby effectively giving even more of the Pacific over to Japanese control. The missing 'third strike' was, perhaps, crucial, and because of this the Japanese really did lose the war at the very start.

Had the Japanese carriers pushed more deeply into the **Indian Ocean**, they could have facilitated the occupation Ceylon and cut British oil supplies from the Middle East by enabling Madagascar to be seized from the Vichy French. The capture of Ceylon, along with her control of Malaya, would have given Japan the bulk of the world's natural rubber supplies. The cutting-off of Britain's oil supplies from the Middle East would have had major implications for that country's war effort on any front, while the Japanese Navy's control of Madagascar would have given it control of the entire Indian Ocean, turning it into a 'Japanese lake'.

the unenviable task of ensuring that the British Empire lost no more territory to the Japanese onslaught, but he commanded a force that was numerically and qualitatively weaker in all respects, and especially in terms of aircraft. That said, following some early tragic losses for the British, it was the Royal Navy that seized the initiative for the first time against the IJN in May 1942 by leading an invasion of Madagascar and turning its very useful port facilities to Allied uses. This denied the western Indian Ocean to the Japanese, and safeguarded convoy routes to and from India and the Middle East. It was another lost opportunity for the IJN. Ultimately, the British would begin their push from the Indian Ocean in 1944 and squeeze the Japanese out of their conquered territories of Burma, Thailand and Malaya. However, in the spring of 1942 the Japanese Navy's attention was far from the Indian Ocean.

In April, the failure to destroy the whole of the US fleet and its base at Pearl Harbor was brought squarely home, not just to the IJN but to Japan as a whole, when the American carrier USS *Hornet*, escorted by her sister-ship USS *Enterprise*, flew off Army B-25 Mitchell medium bombers, led by Lieutenant Colonel Jimmy Doolittle, in a daring raid against the Japanese home islands. Although achieving very little in terms of physical damage, the presence of American bombers over Japan confirmed that the United States was far from being out of the war. This morale-boosting raid for the American public managed to damage the confidence of a number of senior Japanese. Furthermore, a growing number of other smaller carrier raids were experienced by Japanese garrisons on their newly occupied territories, and it was realised that these 'pin prick' raids would continue unless something was done about the US carriers. The failure to catch the American aircraft carriers at Pearl Harbor was appreciated by the IJN High Command, and Yamamoto was already starting to plan an ensnarement of the remaining US ships as early as January 1942. Other, more pressing priorities overcame this plan, but the Doolittle raid in April and the events of the first week of May in the Coral Sea confirmed its importance.

By the spring of 1942, the IJN concluded that the supply lines between Asia and America required cutting, particularly those to Australia, America's forward operating base in the theatre. To achieve this, a decisive move south was required. Port Moresby, at the tip of Papua, was still in Allied hands, and needed to be taken as it controlled the Coral Sea and a further 'springboard': with these waters under Japanese control, Australia would lie open to attack, and a US supply line would be cut. Moreover, ever more Pacific islands would as a result come under Japanese rule, strengthening their crucial war supplies of minerals and materials. However, in the ensuing action to take Port Moresby, the Japanese advance was checked by the American Admiral, Jack Fletcher, and principally by his two carriers, *Lexington* and *Yorktown*. Both sides claimed victory, and in fact both were right. The IJN had won a tactical victory in that it lost only a light carrier in return for the American *Lexington* and the *Yorktown* sunk (although in fact *Yorktown* was badly damaged but still afloat and under her own power). However, the Japanese push to Port Moresby was halted, and the IJN invasion transports turned around, and so the Allies could claim a strategic victory. The Americans also realised that, given sufficient warning and with their assets in the right place (plus a degree of luck), the Japanese could be stopped.

Admiral Fletcher and his task force – comprising his two carriers along with US, Australian and British escorts – were well placed in the Coral Sea as a result of work done by US Navy code-breakers. However, his forces suffered from a number of missed chances and some poor aerial reconnaissance. That said, the damage to the Japanese carriers *Shokaku* and *Zuikaku*, along with the sinking of the small carrier *Shoho* and the loss of a large number of vital IJN air crews, had important consequences for the Japanese at Midway. For example, the Americans were able to demonstrate for the first time that they could hold their own against the Imperial Japanese Navy and its carriers. Secondly, there would be fewer carriers, and fewer of the already dwindling number of very skilled air crews, available for Midway in June. Furthermore, the engagement seemed to show that US commanders, from Nimitz down to the lowest levels, were beginning to grasp what was required to combat the Japanese. Coral Sea was a

The Doolittle Raid caught the imagination of a demoralised American President and people. At the time, it was viewed as a great propaganda success but of little military significance; it can now be seen as an event of immense value as it helped to convince Yamamoto of the righteousness of his crusade against Midway. An Army B-25 takes off from the deck of USS *Hornet*.

Two points of interest should be noted here. First of all, the USN torpedo aircraft were unsuccessful in their strikes against the IJN fleet carrier *Shokaku*. This was a situation that would be repeated at Midway, against the four fleet carriers present. Secondly, the IJN began to retire from the Coral Sea at the same time as Admiral Fletcher began to withdraw his forces. They were sent back in by Yamamoto to find the remaining US forces, only to discover that the US warships had escaped. This failure to press home what was still a numerical and qualitative Japanese advantage would also be seen again during the Midway battle. For example, in an attempt to save the USN carrier *Lexington* from attack, the rapidly dwindling number of Grumman F4F Wildcat fighters were augmented by Douglas Dauntless scout-bombers, but to no avail. The US forces had sustained heavy damage and possessed no reserves. Whilst the IJN had also suffered severe losses, it still possessed a limited capability. However, because the Japanese withdrew and cancelled the invasion of Port Moresby, the Battle of the Coral Sea can be seen as a strategic US victory.

very important battle for the US Navy, not only in terms of stopping the Japanese but in learning from them whilst simultaneously realising that much of their own doctrine – particularly regarding their carriers and air power – was well-founded. The Battle of Midway, and later battles, would prove that the hopes of the Americans in the aftermath of the Coral Sea engagement were not misplaced.

Nonetheless, the Japanese were able to take some comfort. They were convinced that *Yorktown* had been sunk as well as *Lexington*, and on the whole their aviators had performed better than their US counterparts. However, it would seem that battle damage assessments, aerial reporting and observation were poor on both sides during the battle, although the Americans were able to recognise these shortcomings far more quickly than the Japanese. It is interesting to speculate what might have been the situation at Midway had both US carriers present at Coral Sea been lost. *Yorktown* was not sunk, and she and her aircraft would go on to play a pivotal role during the Midway battle.

By the time of Coral Sea, the Japanese naval forces had, as a consequence of almost continuous battles, effectively overextended themselves and had suffered very severe losses, particularly in respect of air crews and carrier availability. These losses would have huge implications, particularly for the outcome of the Battle of Midway. In May 1942, however, the Doolittle Raid, US carrier incursions, Coral Sea and all the other actions of the previous six months meant only one thing: the stage was being set for what Yamamoto hoped, and perhaps honestly believed, would be a decisive battle with the annoying and very dangerous remnants of the US Pacific Fleet. He was going to send almost the entire available battle formation of the Imperial Japanese Navy into an operation that would rid him of the remaining US carriers. A victory would finally safeguard the Japanese home islands from US attack, and give Japan the breathing space she needed to exploit the resources of the conquered territories, stalling any future action in the Pacific by the US for the foreseeable future. It would also meet his desire for revenge against America for her attacks on the home islands in April.

PLANS AND PREPARATIONS
THE PLAN AND THE PLANNERS

There are numerous reasons behind the Japanese decision to engage US naval forces at Midway in June 1942, but perhaps there was one overriding motive – the absence of US Navy carriers in Pearl Harbor. It was these missing ships that worried both Rear-Admiral Nagumo and his superior Admiral Yamamoto, Nagumo because he was concerned with the safety of his fleet during the attack on Pearl Harbor, and Yamamoto because he realised that the gamble to knock the entire US Pacific Fleet out of the war in one decisive action had failed. Had the US carriers been present that Sunday morning, then they would have joined the battleships of the American fleet in becoming twisted crumpled metal wrecks, probably suffering much more than the battleships. Repairs might not have been an option: because of their very lightly armoured decks, US carriers were much more vulnerable to air attack than the battleships, which were designed to withstand gunnery duels and heavy shells.

The loss of the three US Pacific carriers would have changed everything. The American carrier fleet would have been cut in half. Certainly, the US Navy could have brought some or even all of its three carriers from the Atlantic Fleet – as indeed it did – but, with his ten carriers, Yamamoto knew that he could easily whittle down and finish off the remaining US 'flat-tops'. Even if it meant trading carriers one for one, he would have his defensive perimeter and it would be safe for some time, as the US Navy would not commission its next fleet carrier until the middle of 1943. This would give Japan the free hand it desired. Unfortunately for Nagumo and Yamamoto, the US carriers were not present at Pearl Harbor on 7 December 1941, and, as a result, the implications for future Japanese actions were ominous.

It is often assumed that the raid on Tokyo from the decks of the USS *Hornet* in April and the Battle of the Coral Sea in May were the real catalysts behind Midway, but this is far from true. The major significance of these two events lies in the part they played in convincing Yamamoto's critics of the benefits and necessity of the Midway plan, and the neutralisation of the carriers. The reason that the US carriers were not at Pearl Harbor in late 1941 was because they were already in the Pacific, not looking for the Japanese but delivering aircraft to US-controlled islands in order to strengthen their defences against a possible Japanese attack. Amazingly, the USS *Enterprise* almost stumbled across the Pearl Harbor strike force on its homeward journey, but neither side sighted the other. What would become the core of America's defence against the Japanese in the desperate months of 1942 and, crucially, act as the core of the USN battle fleet at Midway remained annoyingly intact.

In the immediate aftermath of the Pearl Harbor strike, Admiral Yamamoto realised that the US carriers and the remnants of the US fleet would have to

Yorktown on fire during the battle following a Japanese air strike. It is quite amazing and a credit to her crew and construction that the ship could absorb so much punishment and get underway so quickly following the first Japanese air strike.

be brought to battle and destruction. He recognised that much of the American strength could, and would, be sapped in the months following the Hawaiian attack as part of the Japanese campaign for South-East Asia. The US Asiatic fleet, along with British, Dutch and Australian ships (the ABDA force) would be despatched to the bottom of the Java Sea by Japanese vessels at the end of February, thereby effectively eliminating Allied naval power in the region. However, the IJN, and

If the US carriers had been at Pearl Harbor and had been damaged in the attack, or if many of the American battleships had escaped damage, then the US Navy may have retained its 'balanced fleet' policy of the pre-war years. America's strategic employment of naval forces could well have been different, and not centred on the aircraft carrier, as was Yamamoto's policy in the first year of the war. The Japanese attack against Hawaii not only shook America but also forced a very beneficial change of operational doctrine on to the US Pacific Fleet.

Yamamoto in particular, had already begun to consider how to orchestrate the *coup de grâce* for the US carriers as early as January 1942, formulating plans that would eventually lead to the IJN and USN meeting at Midway in June and see the legacy of Japanese failure, stemming from the Hawaii raid, come to fruition. The missed USN carriers would become responsible for sinking four of the Japanese carriers that took part in the raid against Pearl Harbor: Japan's missed targets in December 1941 would become her nemesis exactly six months later.

Clearly, Yamamoto is the person most closely associated with the Midway plan. He is credited with conceiving the plan, having recognised the pivotal importance of Midway and the need to destroy the US carriers. Thus he is normally seen as the instigator. He was, however, not totally responsible, nor was he the planner – and he was certainly not, in the end, the executor of the plan. His Chief of Staff, Admiral Ugaki, is often credited with being the real instigator. His belief in moving to the east into the Pacific, in a 'Navy only', operation, is given a lot of credence by commentators. The seeds for this can be seen after Ugaki's strategy for the Indian Ocean was vetoed, not by the Navy alone, but by the Navy in co-operation with the Army. The latter was unwilling to furnish the Navy with the necessary troops, and consequently any thoughts that a few senior IJN officers may have harboured of Japan dominating the Indian Ocean through air power and amphibious operations were short-lived. Therefore, if the IJN could not go west it had to go east, although this is a simplification of the strategy that was put into effect. Neither is identifying the responsibility for the planning a straightforward matter: as with most Japanese planning, Operation 'MI' was a collective effort, for collective reasons. Internal naval politics drove this plan as much as strategic military necessity.

A large pool of naval officers – many senior, many not so senior – can be credited with the inspiration behind 'MI', but particularly associated with it were Yamamoto, Ugaki and the Combined Fleet's Senior Staff Officer, Captain

Kuroshima. In January 1942 the Naval General Staff was approached concerning the initial thoughts on the Midway Plan, setting in train a series of meetings and events which would ultimately, on 5 May, lead to the decision to push ahead with the plan to seize Midway and then engage the US fleet. This had followed the initial approval in principle of the General Naval Staff a month earlier, on 5 April. At the heart of the plan was the seizure of Midway. This would bring huge strategic benefits, such as extending the defensive perimeter being established by the IJN, but it would also act as a 'springboard' for Hawaii, and possibly, from there, mainland USA. Some IJN officers were worried by this plan. For example, Midway was not easily defensible, its size and flat topography suggesting that amphibious landings would be difficult to oppose. Consequently, it could be easily retaken. However, the critics' beliefs would readily be dismissed in the event of a successful completion of the prime objective. Through the occupation of Midway, the Imperial Japanese Navy would finally achieve what it had set out to accomplish six months earlier – the ambush and destruction of the remnants of the US Pacific Fleet. Without an offensive naval capability, the US could not retake the islands, and Japan would be left with control of the central and western Pacific.

This strategic aim – the destruction of the enemy – is fairly obvious and straightforward; less apparent are the political motives behind it. Yamamoto believed that the US was still a threat, requiring IJN action. The Doolittle Raid and the Battle of the Coral Sea demonstrated the threat and confirmed him in his view, providing incontrovertible evidence that he needed a large-scale offensive against the US Navy. His immediate subordinates required a large, set-piece battle to prove themselves to Yamamoto, their Commander-in-Chief, and to the wider Navy; his middle-ranking officers required experience in battle in order to bring themselves to the notice of Yamamoto and other senior officers; and the Navy as a whole needed a major fleet engagement with its US counterpart and the continued expansion of its offensive strategies to counter the Army's successes on the Asian mainland. It would seem that Midway was fated to take place, whether there were external factors or not: if Midway had not taken place in June 1942 then something very similar would have occurred soon afterwards.

The important aspect of the Japanese plan was the seizure of Midway itself – two tiny islands situated almost exactly in the middle of the Pacific Ocean. The US Navy, recognising the strategic importance of these tiny strips of land, would have to despatch its remaining assets there because otherwise the Japanese would take them, position defences of their own on Midway (including aircraft), and deploy around the islands far larger and superior naval forces to any the US could muster. From this point, any American attack could be repelled, thereby achieving Yamamoto's aims.

To ensure success and retain the element of surprise, Yamamoto and his staff created an extremely complicated and what seemed to them all-encompassing plan. The operation to seize Midway would be supported by a series of diversionary raids to draw off any US forces not based in Hawaii. The most important and largest of these raids was an attack on the Aleutian Islands in the northern Pacific. The operation was codenamed 'AL'. In overall command of 'AL' was Vice-Admiral Hosogaya, who was given a pair of carriers – the fleet carrier *Junyo* and light carrier *Ryujo* – to nullify US air power in the Aleutians and a pair of battleships as part of his escort force. The forces involved would be subdivided into smaller units and so would not retain the cohesion of a single large, offensive mass. The attack by Hosogaya would begin on 3 June. Following the destruction by his carriers and ships of American air and sea power (of which there was, in fact, little in the area), landing forces would take the islands, principally Attu, Kiska and Adak. The primary purpose of the attack was to draw off any US naval forces that might threaten the Midway operation. However, it was also assumed that it would focus American attention to the northern Pacific, and with a successful conclusion see further US territory fall under Japanese control, acting as a further demoralising blow to an already weakened nation. On paper, and according to Japanese intelligence, the IJN forces brought together for Operation 'AL' were as strong as any possible US force that it might encounter. In the event, however, they were not stronger, and the Japanese northern force was

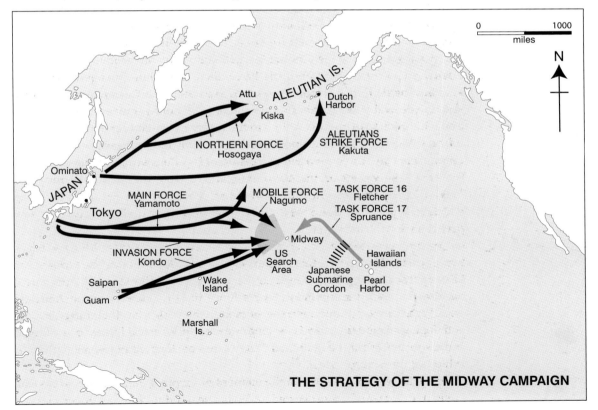

THE STRATEGY OF THE MIDWAY CAMPAIGN

denied the opportunity for total success were it to encounter a US fleet. Either way, the initial timetable for the mission called for rapid success in taking the Aleutians: the northern elements of the Combined Fleet were allocated just over a week to enable Japanese forces to gain control.

However, the main focus of operations would be in and around the islands of Midway. In a very complicated scheme, Yamamoto, rather than sortie as one huge formation, divided up his forces, and further sub-divided his larger elements. On 4 June, Nagumo's First Air Fleet, coming from the north-west, would bombard and neutralise the islands, the strike being flown from the carriers *Akagi*, *Kaga*, *Hiryu* and *Soryu*. Once the US defences on Midway had been destroyed, Nagumo would be free to defend the invasion forces, which would be landed on the 6th. Were any US forces to arrive, not being deceived by the Aleutians operation, then Nagumo would be free to intercept and destroy them. The invasion forces approaching from the south-west would retain air cover from a single light carrier, *Zuiho*, and a number of seaplane carriers attached to the Midway invasion and support forces; further support would be available from heavy cruisers and, as in the Aleutians attack, a handful of battle-ships. However, adding to the complexity of the deployment was the fact that the forces approaching from the south-west were divided into support forces, transport forces, covering forces and a minesweeping force, all under the command of Admiral Kondo.

Yamamoto, however, would not be in the thick of things just yet, as he would be anywhere up to 300 miles behind Admiral Nagumo. He would be commanding the Main Body from his new 'super battleship', *Yamato* (which was and would remain the world's most powerful battleship) together with the rest of the battleships and one small aircraft carrier, *Hosho*. On news from his reconnaissance assets of an American counter-attack, Yamamoto would sweep around Midway, with or without his other forces, to engage and despatch the remnants of the US fleet in his sought-after 'decisive battle'. Acting as his and everyone else's eyes were not just aircraft from his battleships, cruisers and carriers but also submarines on patrol. These vessels would carry out additional reconnaissance, and also act as an underwater 'ambush cordon' between the islands of Midway and Hawaii. In this way, they would be able to inform Yamamoto of US ships moving towards Midway but also help to destroy them before they reached the vicinity of the islands. This cordon would be in place by 2 June. Further afield, a number of land-based aircraft and flying boats would act as extra 'eyes' for the fleet, and, to add just a touch more confusion, a number of smaller, diversionary raids launched from South-East Asia would help to keep the Allied High Command completely off balance – or so Yamamoto and his Chief of Staff, Ugaki, hoped. In fact, having made all these preparations, Yamamoto did more than merely hope: he believed that Operation 'MI' would see the end of the US threat in the Pacific and compel the United States to settle for terms advantageous to Japan.

Yamamoto did not want, nor necessarily like, Nagumo. This must raise the question as to whether a 'Yamamoto man' would have acted differently and been more acceptable to the C-in-C. A 'carrier man' would have been the most obvious choice, and there were candidates, such as Admiral Kurita. Most probably, an officer other than Nagumo would neither have blunted the plan nor been able to re-concentrate the force. By May, Kuroshima's plan had been fully accepted by Yamamoto. But it does raise a much more pertinent question: would an alternative to Nagumo – someone who really understood aircraft carriers – have been more tactically adept at Midway?

The plans were complete by the end of April; Nagumo was informed of them, and the role his carriers were to play, just as he returned from his partially successful incursions into the Indian Ocean earlier that month. There were worries amongst a number of senior Japanese officers, and many of these anxieties were articulated, particularly those concerning assumed US behaviour and the division of forces. However, Yamamoto's momentum had built up, and, upon hearing of dissension from not only his subordinates but also the Naval General Staff, he threatened to resign – on several occasions. By now, however, such was the power of his standing that his position was unassailable, and his resignation was unthinkable. He and his plan stayed in place. Moreover, he displayed a somewhat uncharacteristic attitude for him (and, for that matter, amongst most senior IJN officers) – intransigence and intolerance. However, a number of his subordinates shared this fault, Admiral Ugaki being among them. During the IJN's table-top exercise for the Midway operation in May (it took place during the battle of the Coral Sea) aboard the battleship *Yamato*, Ugaki, the umpire for the exercise, actually became guilty of breaking his own rules, at one point in the exercise famously resurrecting a sunken Japanese carrier in order to prove that point! Such was the determination that this operation should be seen through to a conclusion.

Nevertheless, the idea of the IJN occupying Midway, extending its defensive perimeter and using the islands as bait to trap the Americans has to be seen to some degree as sound. What was far from sound, however, was the planning process, and also the plan itself: essentially flawed, it was to become one of the major causes for Japan's defeat at Midway. It was, for example, vastly over-complicated. The Japanese failed to maintain two of the cardinal rules of warfare: keep it simple, and keep it flexible. They created a plan that was intrinsically complicated and one that, in order to succeed, had to run like clockwork. Moreover, it lacked the flexibility to cope with any breakdown or changes. Although Yamamoto's orders appeared general in nature, they were far from general in reality.

Dealing with these orders were his subordinate task-force commanders. Yamamoto's admirals, amongst whom were experienced, knowledgeable officers, did not feel inclined to demand flexibility as an option following the run-up to the operation. This was partly a consequence of their dealings with Yamamoto prior to the battle. Planning for breakdowns or unforeseen changes would only have been held as further proof of criticism of Yamamoto and

Marines disembark from USS *Pensacola* at Midway Island, 25 June 1942. Admiral Nimitz tried to strengthen Midway for the expected Japanese amphibious assault, but in the event the garrison of US Marines was not called upon to repulse a Japanese attack.

Operation 'MI', and this was, by June 1942, very unlikely. Consequently, at Midway few of his admirals were able (or willing) to think on their feet. These failings came naturally to a number of Yamamoto's subordinates. Some were in high positions, not because of the IJN's being a meritocracy and the admiral in posting deserving of his post, but because of the Navy's appointing system. They had been appointed to particular jobs because either the time was right – it was simply their turn – or due to patronage, not necessarily skill and worth. In a way, both Nagumo and Ugaki fell into this category, and, unfortunately for Yamamoto, both are central to the story of Midway. For without an able, forthright and intelligent chief of staff or senior tactical commander, a commander-in-chief cannot function properly. Either he bypasses the chain of command, which creates its own problems, or he accepts that things will not be done the way he wishes, which creates further issues.

Another cardinal error was the fact that the IJN and the Combined Fleet were divided, not simply split up amongst close-knit tactical groups but, in the case of the Midway plan, divided by hundreds of miles, each component having very different aims. Besides the obvious problems of command and control that this presents – somewhat overcome by the tight 'clockwork' orders – it raises other questions, some straightforward, but others very serious. On paper, the Combined Fleet should not merely have won the battle of Midway, it should have destroyed the US Pacific Fleet: the IJN dwarfed the assets available to Nimitz – eight aircraft carriers (of varying size, but mostly with veterans) compared to the Americans' three, plus a motley air garrison on Midway. The Japanese also had battleships (those remaining in the US Navy were mostly retained on the western American seaboard in case a last ditch defence were required), cruisers, destroyers, seaplane carriers and submarines. In all categories, the IJN was overwhelmingly superior. The question has to be asked: why did not the Japanese Navy turn up *en masse* and seize Midway, await a far smaller US fleet and then crush it? Yamamoto failed to concentrate his forces – an unforgivable error on the part of the Combined Fleet's commander, and one that must rank as one of the most serious in naval history. As we shall see, Nimitz did not make the same mistake.

To compound matters, the plans for Operations 'MI' and 'AL' contained too many assumptions. Planning an operation should involve a combination of knowledge, assumptions and intelligence. The Imperial Japanese Navy, however, based too much of its plan on flawed assumptions concerning US behaviour and on inaccurate intelligence reports. Consequently, and quite obviously, it failed to gauge correctly the US Navy's response. It also became far too confident about its own actions and capabilities, the quality of its intelligence and the safety of its communications traffic. It was wrong in all these areas, and this would certainly force changes on to Operation 'MI' as it unfolded – by which time it was too late.

Crucially, the IJN was convinced that the USN possessed only three Pacific carriers (*Enterprise*, *Hornet* and *Saratoga*), and that only two of these would be sent in response to any operation (*Saratoga* was under repair following torpedo damage). This assumption came about as a consequence of the Coral Sea engagement. The IJN believed that both *Lexington* and *Yorktown* had been sunk. If this were not the case – as many in the IJN believed – it was nevertheless convinced that any carrier still afloat would require the sort of repairs that were slowly being undertaken on *Shokaku* and *Zuikaku*. In many respects, therefore, Nagumo's four carriers did, on the face of it, provide a degree of superiority over their US equivalents – if only just, and only when addressing the US carriers. The US Midway air garrison had not been fully considered: the IJN calculated its strength as being at a much lower level than it in reality was. It was understood that the island's air group needed to be neutralised, but a quick and easy victory here was confidently expected. This dismissal is unsurprising, as encounters between Japanese Navy aircraft and US land-based aircraft had shown the American machines to be markedly inferior.

Another source of misplaced Japanese confidence would be radio traffic. The IJN felt confident that its radio communications could not be read by the Americans. Strangely, however, the IJN were able to pick up and translate certain US Navy traffic but did not feel it necessary to pursue the concept of security for their own transmissions. This failure would allow Nimitz to be given an almost complete picture of Yamamoto's intentions, timings and force levels for Midway and be another critical element leading to the Japanese defeat.

The Americans' plans for dealing with Japan in any conflict in the Pacific had first been formulated in detail during the 1920s. In fact, the US Navy had prepared a whole series of plans, for a variety of contingencies – war with Great Britain, war with Mexico, war with Canada, and even war with all three. However, the Navy's most detailed and best articulated plan was, not surprisingly, that dealing with Japan – 'War Plan Orange'. Although conceived more than a decade before conflict actually broke out, it would form the basis of American naval policy during the Pacific War. Its fundamentals were simple. Japanese aggression would see South-East Asia attacked and mostly overrun. The American garrison in the Philippines and the US Asiatic Fleet would hold the Japanese attack at bay, giving the US Pacific Fleet time to cross the ocean and engage the IJN in a decisive gunnery duel between battleships, supported by aircraft carriers. The conclusion was foregone – an American victory. Events during the six months following Pearl Harbor, however, had not unfolded according to plan. By the summer of 1942, the Philippines had been overrun, the US naval presence in South-East Asia and the Western Pacific destroyed and the US Pacific battle fleet effectively neutralised. Nevertheless, 'Orange' was still the blueprint for America's war in the Pacific, if, of necessity, somewhat modified.

The major difference was now the central importance of the carriers, and, as a result, the newly relegated position of battleships. Furthermore, instead of a decisive engagement off the coast of the Philippines or even off Japan, it was now the islands of Midway that were to become the focal point of battle. Admiral Nimitz, appointed C-in-C in December 1941 in place of the ill-fated Admiral Kimmel, understood the importance of carriers very early on (and, by May, the importance of Midway as well). He was willing and very able to adapt to changing circumstances, showing a flexibility that the Japanese naval leadership was seemingly unable or unwilling to embrace. He was, however, able to benefit from another factor missing in Japan's capabilities – the supply of vast amounts of timely and accurate intelligence from his code-breakers.

The supply of naval intelligence to Nimitz and his battle commanders drastically undermined Japanese plans and assumptions. No matter how precise, ordered and thorough Japanese planning could have been (and in reality it was far from this), the premise upon which all of Yamamoto's plans were based was shattered. Surprise could not be achieved by Nagumo and his carriers; the Americans would be waiting.

The United States began to take an interest in breaking and reading Japanese codes during the inter-war period, although, at times, the aims of the American code-breakers were often thwarted by their political masters and the lack of a co-ordinating intelligence body. There was, in effect, a competition amongst the agencies responsible for overseas intelligence-gathering, and notably between the US Navy and the US Army. The most important result of this was a helping hand in the blindness of Pearl Harbor to the attack in December 1941. Despite this, the Navy had managed to break the IJN's general-purpose code, JN-25, before the start of the Pacific War. The code-breaking needed continually to be updated as the Japanese altered their ciphers, though not as often as perhaps was required.

Japan's inability to achieve surprise was crucial, and the bulk of the credit for this failure is normally given to US Navy and its intelligence service. Naval intelligence has often been portrayed as America's saviour at the Battle of Midway. The traditional view has been that USN intelligence on Hawaii furnished the specific targets, times and force levels of the Japanese operation to Nimitz, thereby giving him the 'simple' task of formulating a plan to ambush the Japanese Navy. This is confirmed by what is seen as a simple but sure-fire tactic initiated by the intelligence staff of the C-in-C Pacific Fleet in Hawaii and agreed to by Nimitz. The US Navy needed to identify and confirm Midway in Japanese transmissions as having the code 'AF' (the IJN had location codes for most territories in the Pacific). US forces on Midway therefore openly transmitted a message concerning water shortages, a problem well known to the Japanese before the war as a result of long-term reconnaissance of Midway and other Pacific islands by their agents. Therefore, there would be nothing suspicious about the transmission. Sure enough, USN intelligence in Hawaii intercepted Japanese radio traffic that incorporated information regarding 'AF' and its water problems. The popular image painted by many since the battle is that this is how all became known to the US Pacific Fleet concerning Japanese plans.

Unfortunately, the impact of intelligence on the US Navy's command structure and its members was not that simple. The Navy in the Pacific did indeed rely heavily upon intelligence intercepts for much of its information, but the commanders still had to make the final decisions for battle, considering not merely up-to-date intelligence but other factors as well. Intelligence could be a double-edged sword. For example, prior notice of the Pearl Harbor attack could have seen Admiral Kimmel move his battleships out of harbor in order to give them a fighting chance at sea. If this had happened, then they might have been sunk in deep water and never been recovered, much like the British carrier HMS *Hermes* off Ceylon in April 1942. *Hermes* was moved out of harbour to save her from air attack, but, as she was in open water when struck by Japanese Navy aircraft, she was lost for ever instead of foundering in shallow water from which she may have been salvaged. More importantly, 'knowledge' of the attack on Midway had been in US hands for some time – in fact, since before the Japanese had agreed to the operation! Midway was so obviously a target and a 'stepping stone' for the IJN that Nimitz and others had already deduced that the islands would be a prime enemy objective as they drove across the Pacific. This opinion was confirmed as an increasingly large number of Japanese long-range flying boats (particularly the IJN's big new Kawanishi H8K 'Emily') began to test Midway and its defences months before June.

What US naval intelligence was able to do was to confirm Nimitz's suspicions and help to illustrate Japan's diversionary manoeuvres. It did not provide a complete picture: fewer than half of the Japanese ciphers were being read, processed and turned into useful information, and in reality only around 15 per cent of each message was proving useful. The rest of the information was being built up through educated guesswork, hunches, former knowledge and other sources of information. There were other difficulties. Transmissions between Japanese fleets were extremely difficult to locate as radio silence was normally practised, but lower-level, less important transmissions could be intercepted, and, from these, more illuminating information than that evident in talk between battle fleets could be garnered. A knowledge of Japanese logistics and assign-ments by the US strategists could enable American code-breakers and analysts to work out the destinations and duties of much of the Combined Fleet. It was this sort of deciphering work that paid huge dividends to the Americans in the run-up to the battle.

By June 1942 there were a number of US intelligence-gathering and deciphering centres in the Pacific. 'Hypo' was based at Pearl Harbor, and there was another in Melbourne, Australia, which had been joined by the remnants of a third station that had been withdrawn from the Philippines during the Japanese advance. These not only gathered and intercepted signals intelligence, but, through their translation and analysis, provided Nimitz and the C-in-C US Fleet back in Washington, Admiral King, with daily briefings and, more impor-tantly, suspected (and increasingly successfully predicted) Japanese operations. In fact, Admiral King had his own intelligence staff, and this team in the run-up to Midway worked closely with 'Hypo' in Hawaii.

The intelligence teams' first major *coup* of 1942 was predicting accurately the Japanese push to Port Moresby in May 1942. This led the US to deploy Allied forces to counter the Japanese southern thrust and resulted in the Battle of the Coral Sea. With their standing proved, the teams were able successfully to convince their superiors about the next major Japanese push, that on Midway. During the Battle of the Coral Sea, 'Hypo' in particular was providing some very useful information. IJN transmissions around Japan dramatically increased – far beyond those required for the Coral Sea engagement. On 7 May the agenda for Nagumo's meeting to discuss operations in the forthcoming battle was inter-cepted. By 9 May Melbourne was passing on information concerning the IJN's 'First Air Fleet Striking Force Order Number Six' and the fleet movements scheduled for later in the month. By 19 May Commander Joseph J. Rochefort,

The Japanese carrier *Ryujo* which was with the Aleutians Carrier Force. She was sunk two months after the battle of Midway by aircraft from USS *Saratoga*.

Secure **communications** are a prerequisite of warfare. A protagonist has to be able to communicate amongst his various elements without fear of the opposition knowing deployments, intentions or capabilities. Modern intelligence services, for the gathering of signals and electronic intelligence (and human intelligence), are essentially a product of the World War I era, but in the inter-war era a number of nations refused to fund them as they were considered 'ungentlemanly', and generally 'underhand'. Others felt confident that their own communications codes and transmissions were too difficult to crack. Bizarrely, the Japanese funded their own code-breakers whilst simultaneously believing their own codes to be invulnerable. The Japanese Army and Navy enjoyed some success at breaking Allied codes, and at the Battle of Midway elements of the IJN actually knew of the US deployments to counter Yamamoto. Although those that perhaps counted most – Nagumo and his carriers – were not to find out until 4 June.

'Hypo''s C-in-C, along with Lieutenant-Commander Edwin T. Layton, Nimitz's intelligence officer, had identified Midway and the Aleutians as the main targets for the Japanese Navy, and three days later Melbourne confirmed that Midway was 'AF' and thus the primary objective. Within days of confirming the target, Rochefort and 'Hypo' discovered the Japanese date cipher used in the transmissions, and with this they were able to work out that Yamamoto would begin his attack on Midway on 4 June. It was with this information that Hawaii was able to begin detailed planning to counter the IJN's thrust.

All this confirmed Nimitz's beliefs and worst nightmares, even if others, notably the US Army in Hawaii and Admiral King in Washington, still doubted that Midway was the target. However, Nimitz had no doubts.

Midway was, after all, America's most westerly outpost in what was becoming an increasingly Japanese ocean, and her ability to defend it was seriously in question. The IJN was an overwhelming force, and, even in the light of the American success at the Battle of the Coral Sea, was still on course to destroy the US Pacific Fleet. American shipbuilding was almost in full gear, but the USN's new light fleet carriers and larger fleet cousins would not be entering service in any useful numbers until 1943. The one clear advantage that Nimitz did possess over the Japanese was his supply of large-scale, useful intelligence. By May 1942, as mentioned, he was in receipt of accurate information showing dates and force levels for the proposed Japanese offensives against Midway and the Aleutians, and, with these benefits to hand, he was able to marshal his forces and put together a counter-plan. Midway could not be allowed to fall. Nimitz had to ensure the Japanese onslaught and advance across the Pacific were, if not pushed back then at least stopped.

At Nimitz's disposal were the carriers *Enterprise* and *Hornet* and the badly damaged *Yorktown*. *Yorktown* was given three days to get herself back to sea and join her sister-ships. Admiral Fletcher was to remain in command of the *Yorktown* and Task Force 17, and ultimately the entire US force sent to engage the Japanese off Midway. This seemed the easier of Nimitz's decisions, but he was faced with a much more difficult one concerning the other two carriers. Until

May these vessels had been commanded by Admiral 'Bull' Halsey, who had already conducted a number of raids against Japanese-held territory, including the Doolittle Raid. He was the perfect choice. However, he was now in hospital with a temporarily debilitating disease, and so unavailable. For Halsey's replacement, Nimitz chose Admiral Spruance – not the obvious choice, but one that was to prove inspired. Spruance possessed a much calmer, more thoughtful temperament than Halsey, which would reap dividends when he was in command of Halsey's aggressive staff on board the carriers during the battle.

With his battle commanders selected and his ships being made ready for imminent action, Nimitz issued his orders. They were simple and obvious. His commanders were to stand off Midway, to the north-east, far enough away to remain hidden from any prying Japanese reconnaissance. From here, and using information from Midway and Pearl Harbor, Task Force 16 (Fletcher) and Task Force 17 (Spruance) would wait until they felt it right to attack. Nimitz gave his commanders the power to act on the spot – something they felt able to do and a policy contrasting starkly with that handed down to the Japanese admirals under Yamamoto. In support of the three carriers would be a screen of cruisers and destroyers, backed up by submarines. Additional support would be provided by an air garrison on Midway that had been rapidly expanded. With these (and only these) forces, Nimitz hoped to be able to check Yamamoto and force him to disengage. To the north he would send Rear Admiral Theobold (Task Force 8) with cruisers, destroyers and submarines, to contest and disrupt the Japanese offensive in the Aleutians. For the defence of the waters between Hawaii and the US West Coast, Nimitz possessed a battleship squadron with an escort carrier (Task Force 1), and the fleet carrier *Saratoga* (Task Force 11), although *Saratoga* would not reach Hawaii until 6 June.

Besides the massive advantage that intelligence regarding Japanese movements, orders and dispositions gave Nimitz, the Americans had made their preparations for the battle with a completely different mindset to that of the Japanese. Few faults can be identified in Nimitz's actions, but, even so, post-combat reports would see the Admiral put forward over two dozen lessons for future American engagements against the Japanese. In stark contrast, the IJN after Midway concluded that there were three.

In general, Nimitz and his planners managed to avoid all the failures that beset the Japanese. He cannot be accused of poor planning, or of overconfidence. The US forces realised what was at stake, and, although the relative success at Coral Sea had buoyed them somewhat – and had given experience to *Yorktown*'s air crews – the reality to the US Navy was very simple. If Nagumo's carriers were to take Midway and destroy TF.16 and 17 in the process, then there was little to stop the activities of the IJN between the Japanese home islands and the West Coast of the USA. Australia would have been picked off, or at the very least neutralised as an offensive base, whilst Japan's exploitation of South-East Asia could continue undisturbed with only the occasional US submarine foray to annoy them. For a year, America would simply not have been able to do anything, and domestic political implications would have brought tremendous pressure on to the US government: the 'Germany first' policy would have been re-addressed, forcing long-term changes on the conduct of the war in Europe and threatening the very future of Britain. The Battle of Midway to the US was not simply about the loss of another American territory in the Pacific: it was a battle to draw the line in the Pacific over which the Japanese were not to be allowed to cross.

To avoid potential disaster, Nimitz required not a time-perfect, vastly complicated plan, but something far simpler, and he was going to have battle commanders with cunning, daring and flair. There would be no division of resources; he would have his forces concentrated. All of America's available carriers, even the battle-damaged *Yorktown*, would be despatched to Midway before the Japanese arrived. Midway's air garrison would be stocked with all available aircraft for offence, whether Navy, Marine Corps or Army. Full use of ships' radar would be employed, as would maximum aerial reconnaissance. If the battle turned against the Americans, it would not be as a result of flaws in planning.

Of the American faults during the battle, perhaps only command and control on Midway, the co-ordination and communication of forces during the battle, increased training and the performance of equipment are worthy of discussion here. These were not simply naval failings but could be applied across the services involved during the battle and could not, within the time-scale to which Nimitz was working, be rectified prior to the battle. As the war progressed, the deficiencies that Nimitz identified at Midway would mostly be rectified for his later 'island-hopping' campaign. These shortcomings, and others, will be discussed in greater detail later.

It was the recall of the US carriers, *Enterprise*, *Hornet* and *Yorktown* and their stealthy withdrawal from South-East Asia that gave yet another advantage to Nimitz during Midway. Here, at Pearl Harbor in May 1942, we see *Enterprise*, previously one of Halsey's two carriers, but now commanded by Spruance, just before the battle.

THE OPPOSING COMMANDERS

THE KEY PROTAGONISTS

In many respects, and as in almost all actions in warfare, the outcome of the Battle of Midway was decided by a handful of individual people. In fact, some commentators would have us believe that it was decided by a few souls well in advance of the battle. Either way, for both the United States and Japan, the admirals and the men under their command in the battle were instrumental in its result.

Many of the characters associated with the Battle of Midway have become legendary. For the Japanese, Admiral Yamamoto, held in great reverence before the battle, saw no loss in his standing afterwards, in the eyes of either the Japanese or the Americans. Today he is one of the few Japanese commanders whom people in the west can name on consideration of the Japanese war effort in World War II, and he certainly ranks as high as Admiral Togo (Russo-Japanese War, 1904–05) in fame. Admiral Nagumo comes a near second to Yamamoto, helped by his portrayal, accurate or otherwise, in various films dealing with Pearl Harbor and Midway. For Americans, the names of their commanders – Admirals Nimitz, Fletcher and Spruance – although slightly dimmer than in previous years, still shine as being names of heroes, gamblers and steady hands and heads, not to mention potential 'lucksters'.

Admiral Yamamoto Isoroku, C-in-C Combined Fleet and Officer Commanding Main Body during the Battle of Midway, has become an increasingly contentious figure, though many still regard him as Japan's most potent admiral during the

Pacific War. He navigated the Japanese Navy through the run-up to war and then successfully saw the IJN achieve victories that were regarded by most as impossible during the first six months of the war. Amazingly, however, from April 1942, he did not win a single major battle (though he did achieve a number of tactical victories during the Guadalcanal campaign), but this has somehow failed to tarnish his image. More incredible is the fact that, besides being the focal point of, and driving force behind, Midway – and therefore the man ultimately responsible for its failure –

Yamamoto, the man who became America's public enemy number one following Pearl Harbor, joined the IJN College in 1900. He served and was wounded during the Russo-Japanese War of 1904–05, and found himself in the United States towards the end of World War I, studying at Harvard. During the 1920s he became a devotee of aviation, and in many respects of America as well. Supposedly a gambler and a drinker, he has traditionally been seen as a friend of America and the West as he attempted to oppose the move to war. His appointment as Commander-in-Chief of the Combined Fleet was as much to do with his ability as with preserving his life in the face of threats from Japanese ultra-nationalists. Yet in the 1930s he was against any further international treaties of limitation, and he was not opposed to the use of the Navy in China or the move south into South-East Asia. Once war began, he was determined to fight to achieve victory. He became increasingly autocratic – a character trait somewhat rare in the IJN of the inter-war years – as demonstrated by his attitude towards the Midway plan. Much criticism was levelled at this plan by all ranks, yet Yamamoto's determination and personality drove it through. Many commentators attribute this doggedness to his anger at the US raid against Tokyo in April 1942, and to Yamamoto's own personal disgust that he was unable to protect the Emperor and Japan from attack. He was certainly a man of duty, but he was also one of increasing contradictions – and perhaps a man whom we will never really understand.

Yamamoto was viewed by Allied and Axis forces alike as one of the IJN's, and Japan's, greatest assets. Accordingly, the Americans, continuing to use their very successful code-breaking system, became aware of his travel plans in April 1943, ambushed his aircraft and shot him down and killed him over Buin.

The commonly held view of Yamamoto is as a leading light in promoting naval air power in the inter-war years. He was one of the major forces behind the acquisition not only of capable naval aircraft for the IJN, but of the best carrier- and land-based naval aircraft in the world. He was, and still is by some, generally seen as a moderate in a sea of Japanese militarists, one who wisely understood that war with America would bring disaster for Japan and only embarked on conflict in order to buy time. He had spent a considerable time in America, where he had studied, visited naval establishments and been posted as a defence attaché. Thus he fully understood the United States' latent industrial power, and realised that, in a drawn-out war, Japan would be defeated. However, a more appropriate view of Yamamoto is of one who believed that, with adequate planning and the daring use of carrier forces, Japan had a chance against the US. He was not averse to war, merely to losing one.

Over recent years, there has been a reappraisal of Yamamoto, and a number of traditional assertions have had doubt cast upon them. This is easily understood when considering his role in the planning for the battle and, perhaps more interestingly, in his dispositions for the battle and his ultimate aims. If he is guilty of over-complication – and of this there is little doubt – then he is only as guilty as most in the Japanese Naval High Command, who also seemed to share this flaw. Later actions in 1944, during the battles for the Philippine Sea and Leyte Gulf, confirm that Yamamoto was not alone in taking simple objectives and giving them little chance for success once a plan had been formulated. What is particularly strange about Yamamoto during Midway was his failure to live up to so many of the traits normally associated with him. His behaviour before and during the battle is much more than simply confusing to the observer. We are told by many that he was a gambler, and this can be seen in ordering the battle in the first place. That said, the Japanese objectives behind Midway – the extension of the Japanese defensive perimeter, the ambushing of US forces, the destruction of the last vestiges of US naval power following Pearl Harbor – were sound enough.

It was Yamamoto's tactical approach before and during the battle that are questionable. He was an aviator admiral, and had been an enthusiastic proponent of naval air power since 1924, when he was appointed executive officer of the Naval Air Training School at Kasumigaura. He had learnt to fly in the 1920s, and in 1928 gained command of the carrier *Akagi*. From 1930 to 1933 he was the Chief of the Technical Bureau of the Naval Aviation Department, and in 1933 was given command of the First Carrier Division. In 1938 he became the Head of the Naval Aviation Department. It was during his time here (and previously in the IJN's Bureau of Aeronautics) that Yamamoto pushed for the design of some of the most advanced aircraft seen anywhere in the world. The Pearl Harbor attack saw him assemble a formidable collection of naval aviators who helped plan the daring strike, including the legendary flyers Minoru Genda and Mitsuo Fuchida. Besides his excellent choice of personnel for the attack against Hawaii, he employed the IJN's six largest carriers in concert in a demonstration of naval power never witnessed before, relegating his battleships to a supporting role. The majority of the IJN battleships, including the huge new *Yamato*, would in fact remain in Japanese home waters for much of the next six months and thereby take no part in any of the victorious Japanese offensives. Yet amazingly, for the Battle of Midway, Yamamoto, utilising many of the staff he had employed for the Pearl Harbor strike, planned to split his beloved carriers into divisions and penny packets. It was his battleships, and not his prized and battle-hardened air crews and aircraft, that he envisaged dealing the death blows to the US carriers were they foolish enough to venture towards him. This hardly made sense in 1942, and it is still no easier to understand today. More importantly, it seems to be very much against Yamamoto's publicly espoused belief in air power. This reversal of behaviour in the Midway plan, perhaps more than anything else, sealed the fate of Japan's carrier forces in June 1942.

Admiral Yamamoto, Commander-in-Chief of the Japanese Combined Fleet, is increasingly portrayed as one of the major culprits for Japan's failure at the Battle of Midway. Many now contend that his emotions and sense of duty clouded his judgement in the run up to Midway. His losses would be compounded further in the actions around Guadalcanal in later months.

If the C-in-C of the Combined Fleet seemed to be undergoing a personality change and cannot therefore be regarded in the same light as the man who saw through the Pearl Harbor raid, what of his subordinates? His commanders would be crucial to the successful execution of the operation, not merely in and around Midway but also during the diversionary attacks in the Aleutians and the supporting activities of submarines and aircraft further afield. The plan, as already discussed, required a degree of timing and precision that was unheard of for naval forces of the day, especially naval forces spread so distantly throughout the Pacific (although there were some areas for which general aims had been given rather than specific orders). Yet this is what Yamamoto wanted. For such a plan to be executed to such an accuracy of timing, not only good luck but tactical commanders of flexibility and excellence were required. Yamamoto's subordinates were from a mixture of specialisations and had varying abilities and experience, although all were men of duty and honour.

Rear-Admiral Nagumo Chuichi, Officer Commanding First Carrier Striking Force, was a Japanese admiral who is almost as famous as Yamamoto. Nagumo led the daring strike against Pearl Harbor, supported operations in South-East Asia and commanded the carriers that forayed into the Indian Ocean to attack British India and the Royal Navy. That said, he is regarded as a 'surface warfare' admiral, who had particular expertise in cruisers (and especially torpedoes) rather than aircraft carriers and naval aviation. He is also seen as a poor choice for carrier group command, owing to his reputation for timidity and inflexibility. Mitsuo Fuchida believed Nagumo to be too conservative, and unable to foresee developments in an unfolding battle. Certainly, since Midway, Nagumo has been berated by many commentators for not seizing the chances he was offered, for not organising his reconnaissance assets properly, and for failing to act against the American carriers with sufficient promptness once he knew of their position.

It could well be possible that Nagumo is a victim of a deliberate bad press and of misrepresentation, and that he has, in part, become a scapegoat in order to cloud, and compensate for, Yamamoto's mistakes. However, criticism of Nagumo is easy to understand. It was he who failed to launch a 'killer blow' against Pearl Harbor on 7 December 1941 and destroy it as a naval base, and again, at Midway, his indecision cost the IJN dearly. Certainly, Yamamoto did not

Yamamoto's apparent reluctance to gamble as the battle got under way is difficult to explain. He was, reputedly, a hardened gambler. He had been with Togo at Tsushima, where he witnessed the skilful employment of Japanese ships in combination with some creative luck. The question that must be addressed is why he did not continue to Midway following the sinking of his carriers. The islands' air garrison had been effectively destroyed, *Yorktown* had been sunk, and the two remaining US carriers had both sustained heavy losses. *Hornet* and *Enterprise* still posed a threat, and an unknown one at that, but the combined fire power of Yamamoto's remaining assets should have been more than capable of fighting through to Midway. The IJN could have seized the islands and then assembled the aircraft being carried on board the ships of the invasion forces for their defence. These would have acted as his air cover, along with newly-arrived carriers either diverted from the Aleutians operation or rushed from the Japanese home islands, against any possible US counterstroke by their last remaining, fully operational carrier, *Saratoga*. Yamamoto, it would seem, at the very moment when he could have regained the initiative and continued through to achieve his objective, failed to maintain both his aim and his morale. These are major failings in a leader committed to upholding the principles of war.

The Battles of the Eastern Solomons (24 August 1942) and **Santa Cruz** (25–27 October 1942) saw the Japanese gain tactical victories but not the decisive 'kills' required by Yamamoto. Nagumo is often blamed for these disappointing results. However, he was not in command. Yamamoto again created complicated ship movements, but at the operational level he gave Admiral Kondo command of the forces, with Nagumo placed under him. Following Eastern Solomons and Santa Cruz, however, Nagumo was effectively demoted, becoming a land garrison commander and later committing suicide in the aftermath of an American victory on the Marianas.

have complete faith in him, and the Commander-in-Chief of the Combined Fleet also knew exactly where to lay the blame for the failure at the Battle of Midway. Yamamoto was quick to replace Nagumo with Admiral Kondo following the sinking of the First Carrier Striking Force on 4 June 1942. Furthermore, following what seemed similar behaviour later in 1942 at the Battles of Santa Cruz and the Eastern Solomons, where Nagumo again commanded carriers and again failed to achieve decisive results, he removed him. Never to command ships at sea again, Nagumo spent the rest of his war commanding land garrisons. He committed suicide in 1944.

Was Nagumo really this inept? Is his reputation fully deserved, and can the woes of the Imperial Japanese Navy on 4 June be placed squarely on his shoulders? The image of Nagumo as the indecisive admiral has remained fairly constant since the Pacific War. It is possible that the commonly accepted opinion of Nagumo – a timid, dithering, technologically backward admiral – was shaped in an attempt to keep Yamamoto's image untarnished. However, and more interestingly, many of his contemporaries viewed him as energetic, professional and talented, and not the admiral popularly portrayed.

At Pearl Harbor, for example, he was urged by his Air Staff to launch a further strike against the US Navy base, but he realised the importance of his carriers and, not knowing the whereabouts of the US aircraft carriers, wanted them preserved for the struggles in the coming months. There has to be a degree of sympathy for this view and for the man himself, even with the realisation of what a third strike against Hawaii might have accomplished. Additionally, he failed to deal the Royal Navy a deathblow in the Indian Ocean, but this failure has much more to do with the decision of the British commander, Admiral Somerville, to disengage in the face of Japanese superiority rather than with a failure by a Japanese admiral to force battle. Nagumo was not present at Coral Sea, and in any case a loss or embarrassment during this engagement was expected by a number of senior Japanese personnel prior to the battle. Concerning Midway, we may find that Admiral Nagumo may have been grossly misrepresented.

Strategically, the Midway operation was, after all, a plan of Yamamoto's making, even if some of the intricacies contained within it were the responsibility of others. Following orders is not the greatest defence in the world, but in Nagumo's case it seems to be true. What worked against him were essentially the plan, the timing and good fortune, and the intelligence the US possessed compared to the intelligence that was not freely available to the Japanese. Critically, Nagumo only had the current Japanese intelligence to work from when he set sail. All of this pointed to a number of conclusions – a huge IJN superiority and a plan that could not fail. Incredibly, information that came to Yamamoto during the battle was not passed to Nagumo; if it had been, the latter's behaviour in the light of certain details could well have been modified. Yamamoto did not

For so long portrayed as the villain of the battle for failing to seize his chances, Admiral Nagumo has perhaps been unfairly painted as a ditherer, timid and unknowing of the ways of carrier warfare. This image has undergone a reappraisal in recent years particularly regarding his reaction to news of US carriers. It would seem that he reacted when he was given the decoded information from his scouts as quickly as possible.

give any clear strategic or operational orders to his admiral, and, in reality, Nagumo had serious doubts concerning the operation, but he did not air them. He had been constantly at war for six months, and this appeared to be taking its toll on him. Moreover, he was not given the freedom to deviate from the overall plan should events require him to do so. He was caught in a contradictory general, yet simultaneously and schizophrenically specific, plan, with his superior far behind him and out of contact. Blame for the failure to have the submarine cordon in place cannot be laid at his feet, nor can the shortcomings in Japanese intelligence during and after Coral Sea.

His actions during the battle, particularly at one very crucial stage can be dissected, but even here conflicting information continues to exist which forces the admission of one crucial fact concerning Nagumo and the battle: it is possible to make only educated guesses about his and his staff's behaviour on the carrier *Akagi*. It is not known what was going through Nagumo's mind, nor exactly what he did for three hours on the morning of 4 June once he had found out that US carriers were present at Midway. Consequently, Nagumo cannot be totally condemned.

Nagumo's missing hours will be explored in greater detail in Chapter 6, along with his deck-handling procedures. There, more questions are raised than answered, and a reappraisal of Nagumo's image will perhaps be required.

Vice-Admiral Kondo Nobutake, Officer Commanding Second Fleet, graduated top of his class in 1907 and was considered to be a brilliant staff officer. Far from being one of the large number of insular Japanese admirals (he had studied in Germany), he was against war with Britain and America. When hostilities broke out, he commanded the southern invasion forces of Malaya and the Dutch East Indies and became typically associated with battleships. That said, he understood the weakness of the Port Moresby operation leading to the Battle of the Coral Sea – namely, too few carriers and too many separated forces. (Ironically, these were also the major flaws of the Midway plan.) In the run-up to the Midway operation, he was one of the few publicly to voice concern, bordering on dissent with Yamamoto, not so much over the operation itself but rather over the sustainability of Japanese forces once Midway had been taken – although it does appear that he had general doubts about the whole plan's viability. During Midway he was ordered by Yamamoto to aid Nagumo's forces once the four IJN strike carriers had been lost, and then to replace Nagumo as commander of the force. Following the Japanese withdrawal, he found himself commanding various naval forces in almost all IJN engagements until after the Guadalcanal campaign (Eastern Solomons and Santa Cruz). He finished the war commanding Japanese naval units in Indo-China.

Rear-Admiral Kurita Takeo was Officer Commanding the Midway Support Force under Admiral Kondo. He was regarded as a torpedo specialist, but at Midway his cruisers did not distinguish themselves, and, following his order to withdraw, two of his ships, *Mikuma* and *Mogami*, collided as a result of a US submarine sighting. He lost *Mikuma* following heavy air attack when he was devoid of aerial protection of his own. He survived the war, having fought in the majority of IJN engagements with the US Navy.

Vice-Admiral Hosogaya Boshiro, Officer Commanding the Aleutians Force (Kiska and Attu) found that he was committed to this campaign for far longer than the IJN or Yamamoto ever envisaged. He fought from early June 1942, undertaking raids on Dutch Harbor, until March 1943, when the campaign was effectively lost for the Japanese. Upon his return to Japan, he was relieved of command for failing to land a reinforcement force on Attu island. Perhaps Hosogaya was ultimately another Japanese victim of the Midway operation.

Rear-Admiral Kakuta Kakaji was Officer Commanding Second Carrier Striking Fleet (Force) during the Aleutians operations. He was an experienced commanding air officer who continued to command carrier groups until 1944, when the Japanese carriers ceased to be operationally viable. Some commentators have put forward the case that had Kakuta been in charge of the First Carrier Striking Fleet, then the outcome could well have been different for the IJN and Nagumo's force at Midway.

Admiral Ugaki Matome, Yamamoto's Chief of Staff, deserves a mention as he represents – much like the admirals above, but perhaps more so – a devoted Japanese officer and supporter of Yamamoto. He was of course also an executor of the Midway plan, if only in the early stages. Opinion is divided as to whether or not Yamamoto liked, let alone wanted, Ugaki as his own Chief of Staff. Ugaki was a determined and loyal officer. He had pursued the normal career path for officers from ship to staff job and back again to ship throughout the inter-war years. By the outbreak of the Pacific War he was an admiral and serving directly under Yamamoto. He remained as Chief of Staff until they were shot down together in April 1943. Interestingly, the IJN Combined Fleet Commander awarded Ugaki a dirk, one of a handful he gave to loyal and trusted subordinates following the Pearl Harbor strike – a strange gesture towards an officer one does not care for.

The Americans could have encountered problems with the chain of command and last-minute alterations had it not been for the determination of the Commander-in-Chief Pacific (CINCPAC) that Midway and neither the Aleutians nor Hawaii was ultimately the target. He was even forced to 'overrule' his superior, Admiral Ernest J. King. King was not just Admiral Nimitz's superior as C-in-C of the US Navy but was also Chief of Naval Operations (CNO). He was abrasive, tough, and not one who accepted traditional norms at face value. However, he was an early supporter of US naval aviation, and a man of vision, which would prove vital to the USN in World War II. At the age of 50, King gained his wings and can be seen as 'mirroring' Yamamoto in terms of the two men's careers. He commanded the carrier USS *Lexington*, the Bureau of Aeronautics and a carrier group during the 1930s. He presided over Nimitz's war strategy in the Pacific but, on the whole, let him carry out 'his' war, although initially he did not trust his desk-bound credentials, only releasing Admiral Fletcher from tactical command just prior to the Battle of the Coral Sea. There were certainly times when the two of them – King and Nimitz – disagreed, as happened during the preliminaries to Midway. In fact, their disagreement concerning the attack

Admiral Chester Nimitz must be seen as pivotal in the American success at Midway. Using a combination of his own intuition and the sound intelligence of Rochefort, he brought together the US Navy's only forces at the right time and place to stop the Japanese juggernaut. He realised the enormity of the task but remained undaunted when he placed his trust in the hands of Admirals Fletcher and Spruance.

on Midway was not finally settled until a wealth of information was used to persuade King of Nimitz's point of view.

Admiral Chester Nimitz came to command the US Pacific Fleet as the long-term replacement for the unfortunate Admiral Kimmel in December 1941 following the Pearl Harbor raid. President Roosevelt despatched him with orders not to return until the war had been won. The new CINCPAC found that his command had been drastically reduced as a result of the Japanese attack on the 7th, but Nimitz shared King's strategy of a tactical offensive, designed to keep the Japanese off guard and eventually bring about a decisive battle when the time was right. The initiative had to be wrenched away from Yamamoto. Nimitz never really got the decisive battle predicted in the US plans of the inter-war years, but he and his commanders won a series of decisive engagements which by late 1944 had effectively neutralised the IJN as a fighting force, enabling the United States and her allies to 'strangle' the Japanese home islands. By the end of the Pacific War, Nimitz commanded an extraordinarily powerful naval fleet, with firepower, mobility and a support train never before seen in the annals of naval warfare. This force, combined with his excellent use of intelligence, enabled the United States Navy to push across the Pacific after Midway and capitalise on its victory of June 1942.

A submariner early in his career, Nimitz was an extremely balanced naval officer and supporter of all naval arms. Throughout the inter-war years, he gained experience of most surface ships, including carrier and battleship operational planning (but not strategic planning), although he never commanded anything larger than a cruiser. Prior to his appointment as C-in-C Pacific, he was Head of the Bureau of Navigation. Thus he came to his Pacific posting from a non-operational position. However, he possessed a calming, confident persona that was greatly to influence his new command. He was a resourceful team player, and this was particularly useful following Pearl Harbor as the US Pacific Fleet was distinctly edgy and far from confident of its survival, let alone its next step. He was able to restore confidence in the Fleet and its commanders. He was especially lucky in having a number of subordinate commanders of great ability, and he was more than willing to exploit this advantage.

He was far from a 'hire and fire' admiral. He realised that individuals made mistakes, especially if they were in positions of importance and stress. However, he would give at least two chances to every officer before he removed him. When he replaced Admiral Kimmel he kept Kimmel's staff, boosting morale. Moreover, he trusted his subordinates and their capabilities. This helps to explain his commitment to his intelligence team, especially that to the Fleet Intelligence Officer, Lieutenant-Commander Edwin Layton, and to Lieutenant-Commander Joseph Rochefort of 'Hypo'. Rochefort was convinced that Nimitz's mind was made up concerning the next Japanese move, and all he and 'Hypo' ultimately did was to confirm Nimitz's predictions and those of his other staff. Nimitz saw it differently, and backed Rochefort in the face of Admiral King's quite public

Admiral Fletcher can perhaps be regarded as the unsung hero of the American victory at Midway. His coolness and ability to delegate under pressure, while realising the vast odds against him and his command, greatly helped in the final victory. His lack of flamboyance, however, has always placed him in a lesser light than Spruance during the battle.

doubts about a Midway operation and Rochefort's abilities in general.

Nimitz was also able to appoint talented people to crucial positions, perhaps most notably Spruance. With Admiral Halsey incapacitated in the Pearl Harbor hospital, Nimitz needed a new TF.16 commander. He respected Halsey's suggestion of Spruance, a man who had never commanded a carrier before, let alone a carrier group. The appointment was inspired. Spruance laid the success of victory for the US at Midway at Nimitz's feet, especially with the C-in-C Pacific's willingness to listen to intelligence, act on it and not be diverted. Nimitz's lauding of Spruance after the battle was a fulsome recognition of the vital role the commander of TF.16 played in its outcome. Nimitz was happy for his commanders at sea to have tactical freedom – to be able to think, adapt and respond. He assigned broad, flexible aims to his commanders, allowing them as much liberty as possible in their interpretation – very much in contrast to the attitude of his opposite number in the IJN, Yamamoto.

At Midway, Admiral Frank 'Jack' Fletcher was in nominal command of the two American task forces during the battle. He was in command of both TF.17 with USS *Yorktown* and of Spruance (with USS *Enterprise* and USS *Hornet*). However, Fletcher's role has been overshadowed by the parts played not just by his superior, Nimitz, but also by his subordinate Spruance. This is unfortunate, as Fletcher's role in the battle is of paramount importance: if any one else had been TF.17's commander, the outcome could well have been very different, and far from the great American victory it turned out to be.

Fletcher's earlier loss of *Lexington* during the Battle of the Coral Sea has helped to lower his profile compared to those of his contemporaries. He has often, much like Nagumo, been painted as timid and insufficiently sharp to command carrier groups. His experiences at Coral Sea and, later, Guadalcanal are both used to support the view that more resolute action could have yielded greater results. However, Fletcher's battles took place in the early years of the Pacific War, during a period when great victories were not yet possible. His success was that of stopping the enemy rather than pushing him back and crushing him, and he is still, unfortunately, often remembered for his 'failures', the loss of *Lexington* and later of *Yorktown*. Fletcher was not a carrier man: he was a cruiser and battleship officer, and seen by some as being of the 'Old Navy' persuasion. This is a little unfair. King is reported to have even blamed Fletcher for the loss of Wake Island earlier in the war. However, in reality, Fletcher

'… set to work to most effectively block Japanese expansion, establish a secure supply line to Australia, and to defend the Midway–Pearl Harbor line. It was a time of confusion, impossible demands from Washington, and of prioritizing. With insufficient strength to reach the Philippines, he diverted those reinforcements to Australia, established a goal to extend the Hawaii–Samoa line to Fiji and planned raids to keep the Japanese away from Midway–Pearl Harbor.'

The raids on the Japanese-held islands of Kwajalein, Makin, Wake and Lea, and the Battle of the Coral Sea in the first half of 1942, all involved the few available US ships in the Pacific theatre, and it showed that the US Navy still had teeth. This, of course, forced Yamamoto into his Midway operation. The USN had to strike at the IJN, but also conserve ships because of their scarcity. 'Fletcher was the admiral at sea that had to execute this policy and to make the decisions to interpret this policy on the spot.'

Thanks to his own style of command, his personality and his avoidance of the Press, **Fletcher's** profile has remained lower than he deserves; indeed, as senior commander at sea at the time, he was even blamed by some for the Japanese attacks on the Aleutians, since they took two of the islands while he was fighting at Midway. However, he was able to calm the fears on the West Coast (and in Canada), although by the time this had been accomplished Fletcher's war services were no longer required and he found himself in command of a 'lesser' theatre of operations – the north-western transport route to the Soviet Union. His command delivered 6,400 planes and more than 150 ships, and trained almost 9,000 Soviet sailors. He was able to raid the Kurile Islands in 1944, repeating the endeavour the following year. In September 1945 he accepted the surrender of the Imperial Japanese Northern Fleet in Mutsu Bay.

Interestingly, it has been suggested that things could well have been very different for the United States had the much more aggressive Halsey been in charge at Midway rather than the 'cautious' Fletcher: it is possible that the US Navy would have lost all three *Yorktown*s in a rush to follow up the first day's action by running into Yamamoto's battleships during the night, as Yamamoto and the IJN had planned. As it was, Fletcher was not a dashing warrior but a task-force commander who shepherded his few resources. Interestingly, Fletcher did not sit for Morison's *History of US Naval Operations in World War II*. This was very much in keeping with Fletcher's character. He was much less flamboyant than many of his contemporaries and saw his part in the Pacific War as a duty that any one asked to undertake would have with little thought for self-congratulation and public recognition. So the US Navy's wartime activities were presented in the first few post-war decades without the benefit of Fletcher's point of view.

On the other hand Admiral Spruance, Officer Commanding Task Force 16, is rightly praised for his part in the battle. He is seen by many as the chief architect of the victory at Midway. His decision – influenced by Browning, Halsey's trusted air officer – to launch his strike aircraft at almost their maximum range enabled the Americans to win the battle. More importantly, his decisions ensured that US aircraft hit Nagumo when he was at his weakest, that is, to hit the Japanese carriers just before Nagumo launched his own strike. Had he done so some 45 minutes later, the Japanese aircraft would have been on their way to the US carriers and the outcome of the Battle of Midway would not have been as it was. Spruance's (i.e. Halsey's) air staff were competent and aggressive, and blessed

Raymond Spruance justifiably ended the war as one of America's most notable commanders. From the outbreak of hostilities, through to Midway to the 'island-hopping' campaign from 1943 across the Pacific, including the Gilberts, the Marshalls, Iwo Jima and Okinawa, Spruance displayed solid and at times inspired leadership of an ever-expanding fleet and in tackling problems of ever-growing complexity. Only on one occasion did he come in for wholesale criticism, and this was during the Battle for the Philippine Sea in June 1944 when he failed to destroy the Japanese carrier fleet sent against him. However, here it was his turn to be cautious – and he was right to be thus, since he was there to protect and escort an invasion fleet and not to seek decisive battle. Nonetheless he was, like Fletcher before him, accused of timidity and of failing to pursue his opportunities. Four months later, at the Battle of Leyte Gulf, the admiral in charge of the US carrier fleet was not going to repeat the same mistake. Here Halsey destroyed the remaining Japanese carriers but let through a large enemy surface fleet that almost destroyed the US invasion forces off the Philippines.

Admiral Spruance is seen by many as the true victor of the Battle of Midway. His decision to launch his aircraft as soon as possible and at their limit of endurance ensured that the Americans struck first in this, the first decisive carrier-to-carrier battle in history. It produced the decisive blow against Nagumo's ships.

with precognition, giving Spruance the perfect platform to strike at Nagumo's carriers.

What cannot be doubted is that Spruance was an intelligent, thoughtful and seemingly imperturbable admiral who seemed to find himself in the right place at the right time. Like so many others in the battle – on both sides – he was not an aviator but from the world of surface ships, in his case mostly battleships and cruisers. Spruance was, however, a long-term friend of Halsey as well as part of his command at the outbreak of war, on board cruisers. It made sense for Halsey, as the senior carrier commander in the Pacific, to put forward Spruance as his replacement for the forthcoming Midway operation and commander of TF.16: what Spruance lacked in carrier knowledge would be more than offset by his own command style, an extremely efficient pair of carriers and some very good crewmen. He was given a chance few are given, and took it with both hands.

Notable among the other key players at Midway were the planners, the intelligence cells and, of course, the air crews serving with both the IJN and the USN, all of whom were instrumental in the outcome of the battle. One Japanese planner in particular should be mentioned. Admirals Yamamoto and Ugaki, and Captain Kuroshima have all been mentioned, but they were not alone, and had large staffs to support them. Commander Genda Minoro is worthy of a mention as an excellent example of a middle-ranking but highly influential, and well known, Japanese naval aviator, who was closely involved in the planning stages of Midway. Genda became a legendary fighter pilot in the inter-war years, creating an aerobatic team known as the Genda Circus. He was an outspoken proponent of air power throughout the 1920s and 1930s and was seen by some as having an unreasonable – dangerous even – 'un-naval' obsession with air power. His view was that, in the future, aircraft would overcome all other arms. This was an extreme opinion for one belonging to a navy that was heavily influenced by the big gun, and yet he partly was right as Midway would help to demonstrate the power of the aircraft in deciding the outcome of battle, and hence wars.

However, steady promotion and experience on board carriers, in training establishments and in China saw him promoted to the position of Senior Air Officer in the First Air Fleet in early 1941, where he helped to create the tactical plans for the Pearl Harbor strike and for Midway, although, owing to illness, he was not actually present on 4 June. He was sorely missed, and his absence is seen as a further reason in a very long list for the Japanese defeat. Genda survived and served for the duration of the war, remaining an ardent exponent and supporter of naval aviation. Following Japan's rearmament in the 1950s, he found himself recalled to duty in the new Japanese Air Self-Defense Force, ultimately becoming its Chief of Staff in 1959, He retired three years later.

A crucial activity for all sides before and during World War II was intelligence-gathering. In the United States, one man's efforts stand out from other significant contributions to the US Navy's large and at times very cumbersome (but on the whole successful) information-gathering and code-breaking establishment. Joseph J. Rochefort was a vital piece in the jigsaw. He joined the US Navy's code breakers in 1925 as a reservist and remained in the field (with occasional short-term appointments) until the end of the Pacific War. He did not look the part of a naval officer (and, more often than not, did not behave like one), which, naturally, made him enemies within what is normally a very conservative service. To complicate matters, he worked for Nimitz although in theory was supposed to report to the Chief of Naval Operations, Admiral King, which made him and his position even more unpopular with some.

Initially, Nimitz was unconvinced by Rochefort's work, his intuitions and his hunches, but he quickly realised that the abilities of this intelligence officer were crucial to the fortunes of the US Pacific Fleet. Nimitz recommended Rochefort for the Distinguished Service Medal (DSM) for his part in Midway, but King rejected the recommendation, reportedly believing that others had played the major part and not Rochefort. After the war Nimitz tried again, and again his recommendation was refused. On the whole, it seems that Rochefort was treated very poorly by King and King's subordinates, such was the power of Rochefort's contemporaries and colleagues, and of the bureaucratic politics which raged from the Pacific to the Atlantic. Yet this one man more than any other enabled Nimitz to move his carriers to engage the IJN at Midway and help turn the Pacific War. A posthumous DSM was awarded to Rochefort's family in 1986(!).

Japanese intelligence was certainly less capable than that of the United States: a great deal of enemy traffic was deciphered, but security was lacking. Japanese codes were changed on a regular basis, but, as the IJN's were being broken regularly, it usually did not take long for US intelligence to read them. Strangely, the Japanese Army did not suffer the same problem, as their codes were much more robust. As well as failures in signals intelligence there were also failures in assessment, as at Coral Sea and Midway. Before Midway, the IJN was deliberately misled by Nimitz, who had Halsey deliberately spotted before he returned to Pearl Harbor. Information such as this would not be available to Nagumo at Midway, and, taken with the generally lower standards of the IJN code-breaking, can be seen as yet another factor working against a Japanese victory in June 1942.

Admirals, planners and code-breakers notwithstanding, the outcome of the Battle of Midway would ultimately be decided by the air crews of the two navies. Had the initial Japanese strike against the islands completely destroyed the infrastructure and the defenders' capabilities, then Nagumo would not have been asked for, nor given permission for, a second strike by his pilots. His aircraft would have been met by US TBDs and SBDs, not whilst in their hangars or on their decks just prior to being launched, but in the air en route for the US carriers. Consequently, Nagumo's carriers would have been less vulnerable, and the US carriers would have been facing a strike by at least 108 enemy aircraft instead of by merely part of *Hiryu*'s air group. On the other hand, without the mistimed arrival of American carrier aircraft over the IJN fleet, the SBD crews could not have planted a 'baker's dozen' of bombs on to Nagumo's 'flat-tops'. The fate of over 200 IJN and USN ships and tens of thousands of American and Japanese sailors ultimately depended on the bravery, skill and good fortune of just a couple of hundred flyers. More specifically, when all other events and characters are taken into account, the battle was decided by a few dozen aircraft.

Until recently, little has been written of the sailors and aviators of the two sides. The common view is that the Japanese were battle-hardened and clinical in their flying, and, on the whole, this is a fair assessment of the IJN air crews. In fact, prior to the war in China, it was normally only a pilot with 500 hours' flying time or more who became a Japanese carrier aviator. The IJN air crews simply trained for a longer period than their American contemporaries prior to 1941 – indeed, commonly for as long as four years – and they certainly had more combat experience. By the time of Midway, US pilots (especially F4F pilots) were slowly catching up with their Japanese counterparts in terms of expertise. It would normally take some 15 months to train a US Navy pilot. Interestingly, and very significantly for the US carriers, the torpedo squadron crews had not on the whole carried out torpedo practice during their training, because of shortages of torpedo aircraft, a telling shortcoming that would come to light in the first six months of the Pacific War. Dive-bombing, however, was an accepted part of operational flying training, and this would stand the US Navy in good stead during the Midway battle.

Both navies had accelerated the training schedule for their aviators before war broke out, and both would use reserves and training staff to plug gaps in numbers. For Japan, this became a very serious problem as personnel normally involved in training would be sent to, and therefore expended in, the front line, creating further training shortages in the home islands as experienced instructors were lost. By the end of 1943, some 7,000 Japanese air crewmen had been lost, many of them veterans and certainly most of the best. It would be difficult to replace them. Average flying times decreased, from 700 hours for a pilot down to 500; by 1943 this figure was less than 300. In contrast, the US naval training programme saw an increase in the output of qualified aviators, while the time spent in the air rose from 300 to 500 hours, and to more than 500 in 1943. Midway in itself may not have been a total disaster for the IJN's naval aviators, but it surely helped to compound the problems facing the Japanese – and the battles that followed Midway made things worse. This led to the bizarre situation that by late 1944 some trainee Japanese pilots were being trained by other trainees.

For the Americans, probably the most famous aviator at Midway was the fighter pilot John S. Thach, although Wade McClusky, the commander of one of the Dauntless dive-bomber squadrons, comes a close second. Thach became a naval aviator in 1930 and, during the next few years of his career, his outstanding performance led to his being assigned as a test pilot and flight instructor. He was particularly noted as an aerial tactician and was regarded as one of the USN's best. When the United States entered World War II, Thach was the commanding officer of VF-3 ('Fighting Three') on board the carrier *Saratoga*. He was one of the few Americans to recognise the increasing quality of Japanese aircraft and the growing gulf in capability between his own machines and those of the IJN. Intelligence reports from the Sino-Japanese war convinced him that the Navy's best carrier fighter, the Grumman F4F Wildcat, was no match for the Mitsubishi A6M Zero fighter.

Amazingly, while stationed on the West Coast after *Saratoga* had been torpedoed early in 1942, Thach used matchsticks to revise the standard fighter formation from two three-plane sections to two two-plane sections – a development that was being accepted as the norm in European and North African skies at this time, mainly as a result of the successful employment of similar tactics as the standard small Luftwaffe fighter formation from the start of the war in 1939. In addition, the two sections were deployed abreast of each other at a distance equal to the turning radius of the fighters. This allowed the section under attack to turn towards the other section, setting up the enemy fighters to be driven off by the latter. This new tactic, called the 'Beam Defense Position' (or, more popularly, the 'Thach Weave'), was tested by Thach and his squadron whilst flying from *Yorktown* at the Battle of Midway and proved to be very successful against superior Japanese numbers. It was quickly adopted as the standard USN fighter formation against the slippery and deadly Zero. Later in the war, Thach was assigned to the Fast Carrier Task Force as Air Operations Officer, where he developed the system of blanketing enemy airfields with a continuous patrol of carrier fighters that was credited with destroying Japan's air offensive capabilities. During the Pacific War, Thach participated in twelve major engagements and campaigns. He would continue his USN career after World War II, commanding carriers and winning promotion to admiral in 1965, two years before he retired as C-in-C US Naval Forces in Europe.

Thach and a handful of others were the exceptions rather than the norms among US carrier air crews prior to Midway. Following the battle, the USN believed that they could match the Japanese in aerial combat, although more work with their pilots and in introducing better aircraft was again confirmed to be necessary.

After Midway, Japanese air crews and many of their commanders generally remained confident of their flying abilities. They had sunk an American carrier, and many of the flyers had actually survived the battle. In fact, very few Japanese aircraft and air crews were lost in air combat. *Akagi* lost three air crewmen in the air, *Kaga* eight and *Soryu* six, although *Hiryu* lost 64 air crewmen in her persistent attacks on *Yorktown*. The aircraft maintenance crews did not, however, generally survive, and this was a major blow to the Imperial Navy's air operations and the manning of carriers in future engagements. Moreover, the IJN flyers were on the whole somewhat dismissive of American flying expertise during the battle, particularly that demonstrated by the pilots of aircraft based

ORDER OF BATTLE: THE COMMANDERS	
United States Navy	**Imperial Japanese Navy**
United States Fleet	Naval General Staff
Commander-in-Chief and Chief of Naval Operations: Admiral Ernest King	Chief of General Staff: Admiral Nagano Osami
	Commander-in-Chief (and Commanding Officer Main Force, First Fleet): Admiral Yamamoto Isoroku
Chief of Staff: Rear Admiral Russell Wilson	
Office of Communications (Op 20): Rear-Admiral Joseph Redman	Chief of Staff: Rear-Admiral Ugaki Matome
Communications Secretary (Op 20-G): Captain John Redman	Senior Staff Officer: Captain Kuroshima Kameto
United States Pacific Fleet	**First Carrier Strike Force** (Mobile Force) and Commander Carrier Division One: Vice-Admiral Nagumo Chuichi
Commander-in-Chief Pacific (CINCPAC): Admiral Chester Nimitz	
Chief of Staff: Rear-Admiral Milo Draemel	Commander Air Operations Carrier Division One: Commander Genda Minoru
Commander Carriers: Vice-Admiral William Halsey	Commander *Akagi*: Captain Aoki
	Commander *Kaga*: Captain Okada
Acting Commander Carriers (and Commanding Officer Task Force 17): Rear-Admiral Frank Fletcher	Commander Carrier Division Two: Rear-Admiral Yamaguchi Tamon
Commander USS *Yorktown*: Captain Buckmaster	Commander Air Operations Carrier Division Two: Commander Hashiguchi Takashi
Commanding Officer Task Force 16: Rear-Admiral Raymond Spruance	Commander *Hiryu*: Captain Kaku
Chief of Staff Task Force 16: Commander Miles Browning	Commander *Soryu*: Captain Yanagimoto
Commander USS *Enterprise*: Captain Murray	**Midway Invasion Force** (Second Fleet) and Commander Main Body: Vice-Admiral Kondo Nobutake
Commander USS *Hornet*: Rear-Admiral Marc Mitscher	Commander *Zuiho*: Captain Obaysahi
Commanding Officer Task Force 8: Rear-Admiral Robert Theobald	Midway Occupation Force: Rear-Admiral Tanaka Raizo
Pacific Fleet Intelligence Officer: Commander Edwin Layton	Midway Close Support Force: Vice-Admiral Kurita Takeo
Station 'Hypo': Lieutenant Commander Joseph Rochefort	
	Northern (Aleutians) Force (Fifth Fleet): Vice-Admiral Hosogaya Moshiro
	Second Carrier Striking Force: Rear-Admiral Kakuta Kakuji
	Commander *Junyo*: Captain Isii
	Commander *Ryujo*: Captain Kato
	Aleutian Support Force: Vice-Admiral Takasu Shiro
	Attu Invasion Force: Rear-Admiral Omori Sentaro
	Kiska Invasion Force: Captain Ono Takeji

on Midway. IJN opinion, including that of Nagumo, tended to believe that the greatest threat came from US carrier aircraft: these had shown their capabilities during the Coral Sea engagement, whereas land-based US aircraft had up to this point not been difficult to contain. In the event, the performance of the garrison-based aircraft at Midway, and that of the torpedo-bombers on board the carriers, did not disappoint the IJN as their crews proved to be the least experienced US aviators during the battle.

Admiral Nagano, Chief of General Staff of the Japanese Navy. Nagano had studied in the United States and became the Japanese Naval Attaché there from 1920 to 1923. From 1941 to early 1944 he was Chief of the Navy General Staff. After the war he was tried as a war criminal but died in 1947 before the trial was over.

WEAPONS AND EQUIPMENT
THE CARRIERS AND THEIR AIRCRAFT,
THE REAL ARBITERS OF THE BATTLE

Midway was the first decisive fleet battle in which aircraft, specifically carrier-based aircraft, were the dominant and decisive weapon system. Prior to World War II, the three major navies of the world – the Royal, US and Imperial Japanese Navies – had all acknowledged that aircraft carriers were important assets in their battle fleets, but only, generally speaking, inasmuch as they acted in a supporting role for battleships. Aircraft carriers were there primarily to provide reconnaissance and spotting for the big guns of the fleet. Their secondary roles were air defence against enemy aircraft – long-range, land-based machines and ship-based aircraft – and anti-shipping strikes in order to cripple enemy ships that their own battleships might finish off in a 'glorious' gunnery duel. By the late 1930s, Japan had also come to see their value in the projection of power ashore. Midway demonstrated that the generally accepted doctrine concerning the use of naval air power was no longer valid. The aircraft carrier, not the battleship, was now the capital ship.

There had been a number of exponents of carrier aviation, and prophets, during the inter-war period, and a series of exercises had demonstrated what could be accomplished if naval aviation were properly exploited. Yet at the start of World War II the battleship or 'big gun' advocates seemed still to be the most influential lobby within navies, and had the dominant voices when deciding doctrine. Certainly, the US fleet was no exception to this, although the Japanese, under Yamamoto, appeared slightly less inclined to adhere to this thinking. However, events from 1939 rapidly changed the accepted doctrine in all navies, and the Coral Sea engagement of May 1942, along with the earlier actions in the Pacific and elsewhere, provided evidence of the changing of the old order as battleships were increasingly shown to be vulnerable to air attack. The ability of a carrier, or carriers, to project power far surpassed that of a battleship or even a squadron of battleships. The Battle of Midway confirmed the growing dominance of the aircraft carrier in no uncertain terms. Just as in the Battle of the Coral Sea in May, neither of the protagonists' fleets at Midway actually sighted each other, with the exception of a handful of submarines; unlike Coral Sea, however, the outcome of Midway was decisive – not just for the fate of the major navies in the Pacific but for the restructuring of navies globally. The aircraft carrier ultimately played the pivotal role for both the IJN and USN, bringing victory for America and defeat for Japan. From Midway onwards, it would be the side with the most carriers and finest naval air arm which would dominate sea battles for the remainder of the war.

As with so many developments the field of aviation, the world's first aircraft carriers were a product of World War I. Having actively pursued the development of aircraft-carrying ships since 1914, the Royal Navy commissioned its, and the world's, first 'flat-top' just before the end of the war. Four years of experiments with seaplane carriers and 'hybrid' carriers – ships able to launch and recover seaplanes and also launch but not recover wheeled aircraft – finally saw the RN arrive at the 'modern' aircraft carrier. The necessity to have available large numbers of reusable, high-performance wheeled aircraft as part of the Fleet saw the commissioning of HMS *Argus*, a converted liner, in October 1918. This was followed by a series of purpose built and converted warships giving the Royal Navy (on paper at least) a far superior carrier strength than any of her competitors, and by the late 1920s she possessed six 'flat-tops'. But by the 1930s it was not the Royal Navy but the US and Japanese Navies that dominated shipborne aviation.

The Anglo-Japanese alliance of 1902–22 saw a considerable amount of British information passed to the Japanese, enabling the IJN to further its experiments with naval aviation, if only very slowly to begin with. However, by the end of World War I they too were building a 'flat-top', *Hosho*. (More than 80 years after the commissioning of this ship, controversy still rages as to whether she was a purpose-built ship or started life originally as an oiler.) The Washington Naval Conference of 1922 ended the alliance with Britain but not the flow of information. Following the Conference, the Japanese Navy converted a battlecruiser (*Akagi*) and a battleship (*Kaga*) into aircraft carriers, giving it three 'flat-tops' by the end of the 1920s. All three ships were influenced by the British, but each displayed Japanese innovations that played a major part in the IJN's future carrier programme. The first three carriers were followed in 1933 by a purpose-built vessel, *Ryujo*. This was an attempt to build a ship below the 10,000-ton displacement limit of the 1922 Treaty, enabling it to avoid inclusion in the Japanese carrier quota. Publicly, it was a success; privately, it was a failure for the IJN, as it had to be refitted with 4,000 tons of ballast and could not embark even half of its intended air group.

Nevertheless, the IJN now possessed four aircraft carriers, and was able to carry out large-scale exercises to prove the versatility and usefulness of their ships. Moreover, the 'failure' of *Ryujo* convinced the Japanese that, in terms of carrier design, size really did matter: small carriers simply carried too few aircraft. What was required was a ship that could carry a squadron each of fighters, dive-bombers and torpedo/level-bombers, plus reconnaissance aircraft and spare aircraft. Consequently, the next four carriers were larger, much more capable ships – *Soryu*, *Hiryu*, *Shokaku* and *Zuikaku*. *Akagi* and *Kaga* were reconstructed in the 1930s, resulting in far larger vessels carrying 50 per cent more aircraft than when they were originally converted. Besides purpose-built carriers, the IJN, recognising the limited capacity and resources of Japan's shipbuilding industry during the inter-war years, had also built auxiliary ships – for example, oilers and liners – that could be readily converted into emergency or 'shadow' aircraft carriers; *Shoho*, sunk

VICE-ADMIRAL NAGUMO'S FIRST CARRIER STRIKE FORCE		
Akagi	**As commissioned in 1927**	**At Midway**
Displacement	29,600 tons	42,740 tons (deep load)
Aircraft	60	91
Gun armament	10 x 8in, 12 x 4.7in	12 x 4.7in, 28 x 25mm (14 x 2)
Speed	32.5 knots	31.5 knots
Kaga	**As commissioned in 1928**	**At Midway**
Displacement	29,600 tons	43,650 tons
Aircraft	60	66 plus reserves
Gun armament	10 x 8in, 12 x 4.7in	16 x 5in, 26 x 25mm (13 x 2)
Speed	27.5 knots	28.5 knots
Hiryu	**As commissioned in 1939**	**At Midway**
Displacement	21,900 tons	21,900 tons
Aircraft	64 (max. 73)	64 (max. 73)
Gun armament	12 x 5in, 28 x 25mm (14 x 2)	12 x 5in, 28 x 25mm (14 x 2)
Speed	34.5 knots	34.5 knots
Soryu	**As commissioned in 1937**	**At Midway**
Displacement	19,800 tons	19,800 tons
Aircraft	63 (max. 71)	63 (max. 71)
Gun armament	12 x 5in, 28 x 25mm (14 x 2)	12 x 5in, 28 x 25mm (14 x 2)
Speed	34.5 knots	34.5 knots

at Coral Sea, and *Junyo* and *Zuiho*, employed during the Aleutians campaign, were such ships.

By the time of the outbreak of the Pacific War, it seemed that Japanese carrier doctrine was much more advanced than that of either the Americans or the British. In many ways this was true. The IJN had built up a wealth of knowledge concerning naval aviation during their campaign against China from 1937, in terms not only of aircraft technology and deck operations but also of the employment of the carriers themselves. Groups of carriers, at least two forming a carrier division, seemed to the IJN to be the most potent form of naval power. This was demonstrated on a grand scale by the Pearl Harbor raid, when three carrier divisions (i.e., six carriers) were employed against the US Fleet, and two further divisions (four carriers) were used in South-East Asia. Even the name, 'Combined Fleet', suggested the importance of carrier aviation, the IJN's battleship fleet and carrier fleet working in concert to form a potent striking force, even though the importance and power of the carrier were far from universally accepted by some Japanese admirals.

From Pearl Harbor onwards, Imperial Japanese Navy carriers were in almost constant use against Allied ships and land targets, in support of amphibious operations and neutralising the enemy around South-East Asia and in the Indian Ocean. They were battle-hardened but at the same time increasingly weary through constant action and the sustenance of heavy losses in aircraft, sometimes for very little gain (as, for example, in the Indian Ocean raid and the attacks on Darwin). However, the carrier commanders and crews did not doubt their capabilities. Nagumo did not doubt them either; having early on been a sceptical advocate of naval air power, he was now, by the spring of 1942, sharing the confidence of his crews in his First Carrier Striking Fleet of *Akagi*, *Kaga*, *Hiryu* and *Soryu*.

The carriers of the IJN represented Japan's best striking and defensive asset, but, even so, they were not performing at their optimum level. Deck-handling

THE AIRCRAFT COMPLEMENTS FOR NAGUMO'S SHIPS AT MIDWAY	
Akagi	21 Mitsubishi A6M2 fighters, 21 Aichi D3A1 dive-bombers, 21 Nakajima B5N2 torpedo-bombers
Kaga	21 Mitsubishi A6M2, 21 Aichi D3A1, 30 Nakajima B5N2
Hiryu	21 Mitsubishi A6M2, 21 Aichi D3A1, 21 Nakajima B5N2
Soryu	21 Mitsubishi A6M2, 21 Aichi D3A1, 21 Nakajima B5N2, 4 Yokosuka D4Y1-C reconnaissance aircraft

procedures could be described as laboured in terms of arming and refuelling (aircraft were usually struck below to rearm and refuel), and although flying operations – both launches and recoveries – could be undertaken at night, this capability was never exploited enough to give the IJN this added advantage. The design and construction of the ships also had weaknesses, particularly regarding the converted merchant and auxiliary vessels. For the vessels at Midway under Nagumo, however, the most important deficiencies are often seen as inadequate anti-aircraft artillery, poor damage control, their lack of radar and, amazingly, a far-from-full complement of aircraft. All four of these failings would prove damaging to the First Striking Fleet at Midway. That said, Nagumo's four aircraft carriers were a very powerful force, hardened, professional and looking forward to battle.

The design of *Hiryu* and her sister-ship *Soryu* formed the basis for a number of Japanese carriers that followed. *Hiryu* acquitted herself well during the battle, but unfortunately her efforts were in vain. On the whole the ships were powerful but too lightly constructed to take much punishment, as the battle would demonstrate.

After World War I the Japanese chose to convert the incomplete battlecruiser *Akagi* into an aircraft carrier and she was commisioned in 1927.

ALEUTIANS CARRIER FORCE		
Junyo	**As commissioned in 1942**	**At Midway**
Displacement	26,950 tons	26,950 tons
Aircraft	53	53
Gun armament	12 x 5in, 24 x 25mm (8 x 3)	12 x 5in, 24 x 25mm (8 x 3)
Speed	25 knots	25 knots
Ryujo	**As commissioned in 1933**	**At Midway**
Displacement	8,000 tons	13,650 tons
Aircraft	48	33 (A6M and B5N)
Gun armament	12 x 5in, 24 x 13.2mm	4 x 5in, 22 x 25mm (2 x 2, 6 x 3) 24 13.2mm
Speed	29 knots	29 knots
MIDWAY INVASION CARRIER (AMPHIBIOUS TRANSPORT FORCE)		
Zuiho	**As commissioned in 1941**	**At Midway**
Displacement	14,200 tons	14,200 tons
Aircraft	30	30
Gun armament	8 x 5in (4 x 2), 8 x 25mm (4 x 2)	8 x 5in (4 x 2), 8 x 25mm (4 x 2)
Speed	28.2 knots	28.2 knots
YAMAMOTO'S CARRIER IN THE MAIN BODY		
Hosho	**As commissioned in 1922**	**At Midway**
Displacement	10,000 tons	10,000 tons
Aircraft	21	11 (B5N)
Gun armament	4 x 5.5in, 2 x 80mm	16 x 25mm (8 x 2)
Speed	25 knots	25 knots

Yamamoto had other carriers at his disposal for the operation, and he would deploy four of these during the battle – *Hosho*, to provide reconnaissance (and a very limited striking force) for his main body, *Zuiho*, to provide fighter escort and an attack capability for the actual Midway invasion force, and *Junyo* and *Ryujo*, which were to spearhead the Aleutians attack. All of these were smaller carriers, especially *Hosho*, which could operate fewer than a dozen aircraft. Nonetheless, *Ryujo* and *Junyo* could carry a useful air group (the latter embarked 53 aircraft) and would be sorely missed by Nagumo during Midway.

This was a sizeable number of carriers, dwarfing the number available to the US Navy, which could muster only five fleet and one light aircraft carrier when the Pacific and Atlantic Fleets were combined. The Japanese also possessed a large number of seaplane carriers. Seaplanes were regarded as reconnaissance platforms and were normally carried in small numbers by cruisers and battle-ships. The IJN, however, also employed large numbers of fighter seaplanes and grouped these together on a number of their seaplane carriers as well as basing them across the Pacific for island defence. They could prove useful against lumbering long-range, land-based aircraft and, at times, against more nimble machines. In fact, Yamamoto deployed what could have been two very useful seaplane carriers with large numbers of aircraft with the invasion forces – *Chitose* and *Kamikawa Maru* – but they played only a small part in the battle.

The Americans and Japanese had followed very similar evolutionary processes in the introduction of aircraft carriers to service. Like the Japanese *Hosho*, the US Navy's first carrier, the USS *Langley* (a small converted collier), was commissioned at about the time of the Washington Conference. Like *Hosho*, she provided essential training for America's fledgeling carrier aviators. She was followed by two post-Washington battlecruiser conversions, *Lexington* and *Saratoga*, which were commissioned later in the 1920s. These were the 'super carriers' of their day. Of immense size compared to other carriers, they could each, in theory, carry over 90 aircraft, although operational considerations usually kept this figure lower. Like the Japanese in the early 1930s, the US exper-imented with a smaller, purpose-built carrier, USS *Ranger*, but, as with *Ryujo*, she was found to be too small to be practical and, like the Japanese, the USN decided on bigger ships – the famous *Yorktown* class. Experience with *Ranger* was not completely wasted as her design would heavily influence America's new carriers, *Yorktown*, *Enterprise*, *Hornet* and *Wasp*, before Pearl Harbor.

By the late 1930s the USN also shared the belief in the necessity of having dedicated aircraft on board their carriers in order to fulfil specific roles. More importantly, because of their large size, they could carry large air groups. Thus on board an American carrier could be found a fighter squadron, a dive-bomber squadron, a torpedo-bomber squadron and a squadron of scout/dive-bomber aircraft for reconnaissance, plus spare aircraft. Although US carriers had a high degree of offensive power, they were seen very much as a support tool for the fleet – to the point that, by the late 1930s, the US Navy was considering the omission of torpedo-bombers, a key component of a carrier's offensive inventory, from their air groups altogether. The US carriers had, during exercises in the inter-war period, demonstrated their deadly capability, but prior to the outbreak of war the three Pacific Fleet carriers found themselves attached to three surface-action groups headed by battleships, confirming that, at the start of December 1941, the 'big gun' lobby held sway in the US Navy.

Things changed following the neutralisation of the US Pacific Fleet battleships, forcing the USN to use their only remaining surface offensive forces – their carriers – against the Japanese. The ships were employed by Nimitz as 'hit-and-run' attackers and then as the only bulwark against further Japanese aggression, as during the Battle of the Coral Sea. *Lexington* was lost in this engagement, whilst her sister-ship, *Saratoga*, had been damaged earlier in a submarine attack. *Langley* was

Yorktown Class	As commissioned in 1937	At Midway
Displacement	19,800 tons standard	27,500 tons full load
Aircraft	80 max.	75–80
Gun armament	8 x 5in, 16 x 1.1in	8 x 5in, 16 x 1.1in
	(4 x 4), 16 x 0.5in	(4 x 4), 16 x 0.5in
Speed	33 knots	33 knots
Aircraft carried:		

Yorktown: 25 (VF-3) Grumman F4F Wildcat fighters, 19 (VS-3) plus 18 (VB-5) Douglas SBD Dauntless dive-bombers, 13 (VT-3) Douglas TBD Devastator torpedo-bombers
Enterprise: 27 (VF-6) F4F, 19 (VS-6) plus 19 (VB-6) SBD, 14 (VT-6) TBD
Hornet: 27 (VF-8) F4F, 19 (VS-8) plus 19 (VB-8) SBD, 15 (VT-8) TBDs

sunk by Japanese bombers while acting as an aircraft transport off Java in February 1942. *Ranger* and *Wasp* were with the US Atlantic Fleet, aiding the British, leaving only the three *Yorktown*s to combat the Japanese onslaught in early June 1942. The *Yorktown*s would prove to be robust vessels, capable of taking much more punishment than they were designed to take, and *Enterprise* survived the war to see the Japanese surrender. They would form the basis of the *Essex* class carriers, the first of which were laid down following President Roosevelt's Naval Acts of 1940. The *Essex*es eventually formed the backbone of the US Pacific Fleet, which was used so successfully in the offensives across the Pacific from 1943 onwards.

On paper, Yamamoto's force dwarfed that of Nimitz's and his admirals off Midway – eight aircraft carriers deployed by the Japanese versus just three American. In all other categories of ship, the American fleet also fell well below the strengths deployed by the IJN. Yamamoto deployed eleven battleships to the US Navy's none (although a battleship squadron was located off the US West Coast), and in cruisers, destroyers and all other vessels the IJN's numbers far exceeded those of the USN (as can be seen in the box on the opposite page).

This extremely impressive Japanese line-up was disjointedly spread across the northern and central Pacific in accordance with an over-complicated and presumptuous plan. The US Navy, however, concentrated its forces as much as possible, especially with regard to the 'fast task force' concept, first practised during 1942 at Midway.

A number of points are raised by the opposing orders of battle. First, the Japanese forces used in the Aleutians diversionary campaign were significant in scale, with two aircraft carriers and four battleships employed along with a host of other vessels. Nimitz, knowing that the Aleutians raid was a diversion, nevertheless despatched a large and potentially vital portion of his fleet, except, of course, a carrier. Secondly, in terms of sheer numbers, the air assets of the Americans on and around Midway considerably exceeded those of Nagumo's First Carrier Striking Fleet. Were the land-based and carrier-based air groups to work together and co-ordinate their attacks against the Japanese, Nagumo's chances of success would have been markedly lowered. As it was, they did not co-ordinate their attacks, partly because of command and control issues but also because radio silence was supposedly being maintained. Even so, the Japanese fleet at Yamamoto's command was still large, if very thinly and diversely spread. Ultimately, it would be a question of whoever got the 'killer blows' in first would decide the fate of the battle.

IMPERIAL JAPANESE NAVY ORDER OF BATTLE FOR MIDWAY AND THE ALEUTIANS	
Operation 'MI' Commanded by Admiral Isoroku Yamamoto. In command of the Main Force (First Fleet) under Admiral Yamamoto: 3 battleships: *Yamato, Nagato, Mutsu* 1 carrier: *Hosho* (11 B5N2/B5N1, possibly some A5M) 2 seaplane carriers (no aircraft, 12 midget submarines, 5 MTBs) 1 light cruiser: *Sendai*　　9 destroyers 2 oilers　　1 rescue ship	**Aleutian Force/Northern Force (Operation 'AL').** Commanded by Vice-Admiral Moshiro Hosogaya. In charge of the Northern Force Main Body under Vice-Admiral Hosogaya 1 heavy cruiser: *Nachi* (3 seaplanes) 2 destroyers　　2 oilers　　3 cargo ships
First Carrier Striking Fleet (or Striking Force or First Air Fleet or Mobile Force) under Vice-Admiral Nagumo 4 carriers: *Akagi, Kaga, Hiryu, Soryu* (263 A6M, B5N, D3A) 2 battleships: *Haruna, Kirishima* (3 seaplanes each) 2 heavy cruisers: *Tone, Chikuma* (5 seaplanes each) 1 light cruiser: *Nagara* 12 destroyers　　5 oilers	**Second Carrier Striking Force under Rear-Admiral Kakuta** 2 carriers: *Junyo* (24 A6M2, 21 D3A1), *Ryujo* (16 A6M, 21 B5N2) 2 heavy cruisers: *Maya, Takao* (3 seaplanes each) 3 destroyers　　1 oiler
Midway Close Support Force under Vice-Admiral Kurita 4 heavy cruisers: *Kumano, Suzuya, Mogami, Mikuma* (12 seaplanes) 2 destroyers　　1 oiler	**Midway Invasion Force (Second Fleet and Main Body) under Vice-Admiral Nobutake Kondo** 1 carrier: *Zuiho* (12 A6M2, 12 B5N2) 2 battleships: *Kongo, Hiei* (3 seaplanes each) 4 heavy cruisers: *Atago, Chokai, Myoko, Haguro* (10 seaplanes) 1 light cruiser: *Yura*　　8 destroyers 4 oilers　　1 rescue ship　　1 repair ship
Midway (and Kure) Occupation Force under Rear-Admiral Tanaka 2 seaplane carriers: *Chitose* (16 A6M2-N 'Rufe', 4 scouts), *Kamikawa* (8 A6M2-N 'Rufe', 4 scouts) 12 destroyers　　4 patrol boats 12 transports (5,000 troops)　　1 oiler	**Aleutian Support Force under Vice-Admiral Takasu** 4 battleships: *Hyuga, Ise, Fuso, Yamashiro* 2 light cruisers: *Kitikami, Oi* 12 destroyers　　2 oilers
Minesweeper Group under Captain Miyamoto 4 minesweepers　　3 submarine-chasers 1 supply ship　　2 cargo ships	**Attu Invasion Force under Rear-Admiral Omori** 1 light cruiser: *Abukuma*　　4 destroyers 1 minelayer　　1 transport
Midway Advanced Submarine Force under Vice-Admiral Komatsu (at Kwajalein) 10 submarines	**Kiska Invasion Force under Captain Ono** 2 light cruisers: *Kiso, Tama* (2 seaplanes) 1 auxiliary cruiser/armed merchant ship 3 destroyers　　2 transports　　3 minesweepers
Land-based air force (11th Air Fleet) More than 40 flying boats, 70 A6Ms and 70 B5N2s based at Jaluit, Wotje and Kwajalein were at Yamamoto's disposal. Additionally, the Japanese fleet carried 36 A6Ms for the future Midway garrison.	**Aleutians Advanced Submarine Force under Rear-Admiral Yamazaki** 6 submarines

In many respects, the IJN and USN had similar aircraft, carrying out similar roles, on board their carriers. It is fair to say, however, that the Japanese had the benefit of experienced air crews and ground crews, and a definite if slight edge in aircraft technology.

US PACIFIC FLEET ORDER OF BATTLE FOR THE DEFENCE OF MIDWAY AND THE ALEUTIANS	
Task Force 17 under Rear-Admiral Fletcher	**Aleutians (Northern) air assets**
1 carrier: *Yorktown* (71 F4F, SBD, TBD)	The US possessed over 100 fighters (P-36, P-39, P-38, P-40),
2 cruisers: *Astoria*, *Portland* (4 seaplanes)	20 PBY and in excess of 50 bombers (B-17, B-18, B-24, B-26)
6 destroyers	in their northern territories – effectively, a mixture of old and
	new.
Task Force 16 under Rear-Admiral Spruance	**Midway Garrison under Captain Simard USN, C-in-C NAS**
2 carriers: *Enterprise*, *Hornet* (150 F4F, SBD, TBD)	**Midway, with Colonel Shannon (Sand Island), Major**
5 heavy cruisers: *New Orleans*, *Minneapolis*, *Vincennes*,	**Benson (Eastern Island) and Lieutenant-Colonel Kimes**
Northampton, *Pensacola*	**(Marine Aircraft Group 22)**
1 anti-aircraft cruiser: *Atlanta* (17 seaplanes)	11 MTBs (MTB Squadron 1)
11 destroyers 2 oilers	26 PBY (VP-23, VP-44)
	6 TBF (VT-8)
Task Force 8 under Rear-Admiral Theobald	20 F2A, 6 F4F (VMF-221)
5 heavy cruisers: *Nashville*, *Indianapolis*, *Louisville*, *St Louis*,	16 SBD, 16 SB2U (VMSB-241)
Honolulu (20 seaplanes)	4 B-26, 16 B-17 (7th AAF detachment)
13 destroyers 6 submarines	Almost 3,500 USN, USMC and USAAF personnel
2 oilers 1 transport	

Fighter aircraft were, of course, first developed during World War I. Land-based and ship-based aircraft were initially seen as great advances in terms of reconnaissance and the provision of accurate spotting for the guns of armies and navies. However, one country's advantage was another's disadvantage, and, besides carrying out reconnaissance, it was important that one's opponent was prevented from doing likewise. Thus was born, in 1915, the scout, which saw hand-held guns and, at times, more medieval weapons added to the aircraft. Soon purpose-built fighter aircraft were joining the ranks of the air services. These were used either to escort reconnaissance machines or simply to 'sweep' away enemy aircraft in an attempt to gain a nominal control of the air.

By 1918, the world's fighter aircraft looked remarkably alike – fabric-covered biplanes with speeds of up to 100–120mph and fixed undercarriages, each aircraft having two light machine guns firing forward. This basic concept remained much the same during the 1920s and into the 1930s, with only speeds, creeping up to 200mph, making progress. Air forces around the world were remarkably conservative in what they wanted – essentially a nimble, dog-fighting machine, with which latter-day knights of the sky could joust against their opponents. However, fighter aircraft began to change from the mid 1930s with the introduction of stressed-skin, metal monoplanes with retractable undercarriages and speeds approaching and even surpassing 300mph. Moreover, many were no longer equipped with merely two machine guns but instead a larger number of guns and, in some instances, heavy-calibre cannon as well. All these innovations served to give notice of a new power in the sky.

The Japanese Navy was at the forefront of these developments, recognising that quality could act as a 'force multiplier' for its numerically weaker forces –

an opinion shared and promoted by Yamamoto. In 1935, the IJN flew the world's first carrier-based monoplane fighter, the Mitsubishi A5M ('Claude'), and in 1939 followed this up with the Mitsubishi A6M Zero-sen, or Zero ('Zeke' or 'Hamp') to the Allies. The Zero would be manufactured in numbers greater than those of any other Japanese aircraft during the war, over 10,000 being produced from between 1940 and 1945. The A6M had incredible range and manoeuvrability, together with the firepower of two machine guns and two cannon and a top speed of 316mph (for an A6M2 present at Midway). Not only was it a revolutionary carrier fighter: in theory, it could hold its own against any land or carrier-based fighter aircraft in the world in 1939. Traditionally, carrier-

Had all the IJN battleships, carriers and other surface ships involved in the Midway operation been concentrated and located together, the fighting cohesion of this immense naval unit would have been vastly improved and probably unstoppable. The battleships, in particular, could have proved very useful, acting as escorts for the carriers – and as extra targets, perhaps decoying away a number of attacking US aircraft (although orders to US pilots concerning their targets were specific). The anti-aircraft firepower of the Japanese battleships was considerable. The USN later in the war would use their battleships as floating anti-aircraft batteries, providing walls of shells against incoming Japanese aircraft and protecting the US carriers. Had this role been assigned to his battleships by Yamamoto in June 1942, the Japanese would have stood a better chance of retaining their carriers and turning the battle.

based aircraft had been seen as inferior to their land-based cousins, but the Zero broke the mould. More famously, it would also go on to break the back of the Allied fighter units in the first year of the Pacific War. However, the designer of the A6M, the brilliant Jiro Horikoshi, had been working to very tight naval specifications. These had evolved from the combat experience of the naval flyers over China since the start of the 'China Incident' in 1937. To achieve success for Mitsubishi in the fighter selection process, and to meet the tight specifications imposed on him, Horikoshi was forced to delete a number of items from his aircraft – items which, by the time of World War II, would be considered in the West as necessary features of a modern combat aircraft, notably armour for the pilot and self-sealing tanks for his machine. In addition, Horikoshi made the airframe so light in order to achieve the manoeuvrability required with the low-powered engines then available that the Zero was a remarkably fragile aircraft, a characteristic that Allied pilots would confirm if they landed their shells on target during the early years of the Pacific War. On the other hand, Horikoshi introduced a remarkable number of innovations with the Zero, particularly the use of drop tanks (sometimes made from wood and paper) in order to extend its already considerable range.

To counter this Japanese advance in fighter design, and to modernise its own rather antiquated fleet of biplanes, the US Navy had begun to introduce its own stressed-skin monoplanes by 1940. The first of these was the Brewster F2A Buffalo, a short, squat, unremarkable little aircraft that rarely flew from

The names 'Val', 'Kate' and 'Zeke' appear frequently within this book and others. These are names synonymous with Japan's war effort, yet they must strike many who come across them for the first time as being strange appellations for combat aircraft. Why call a Navy bomber – a bringer of death to ships – 'Kate' or 'Val'? Would anyone today relish being shot down by a 'George', a 'Zeke' or a 'Hamp', or indeed an Army 'Oscar' or 'Frank'? These names were simply part of an effective reporting system developed by the Allies in 1942 for easy recognition of the myriad Japanese aircraft, of both the Army and the Navy, that were being encountered. Knowledge of Japanese aircraft was at best patchy, owing partly to Japanese government secrecy concerning their aircraft industry and partly to what appeared to be complicated official Japanese designations but also because the Western allies had committed the grave error of ignoring and underestimating Japanese technology. As one journalist authoritatively wrote prior to Pearl Harbor, the 'Japanese fly antiquated aircraft from a handful of aircraft carriers and never at night.' This was an attitude that was to cost the Allies dear in the six months following 7 December 1941.

The reporting system was devised primarily by Captain Frank T. McCoy USAAF and Technical Sergeant Francis M. Williams USAAF in July 1942 – a month after the Battle of Midway – whilst based in Australia. In fact, the system was not in full use by the Allies until 1943. Consequently, the names applied to aircraft at Midway are in fact 'after-battle' names and were not used at the time. 'Zero' was the Japanese name for the Mitsubishi A6M as it referred to the first year of its manufacture, the Japanese year 2600 (1940), and was thus a Type '0' Navy fighter. The system was simple. All fighters were given masculine names, initially from McCoy's state of Tennessee (thus 'Zeke' and 'Rufe'), whilst bombers and flying boats had feminine names (such as 'Betty', 'Kate' and 'Emily'). The sources for the names varied, and a number had links to relatives and friends of McCoy and Williams. For example, 'Val' (Aichi D3A) was the name of an Australian army sergeant, and a friend of the supervisor! The system was applied to both Navy and Army aircraft.

carriers. At the start of the Pacific campaign the F2A formed the backbone of many American naval units and also the British and Dutch fighter squadrons in South-East Asia, but by the time of Midway they could only be found flying from land bases in Marine Corps colours. The performance of the Buffalo – as the name suggests – was generally lacklustre, even in the hands of experienced pilots, a problem compounded for the Americans in June 1942 because there were few such pilots in any case. On the other hand, the Navy did have a much more promising aircraft in the form of the Grumman F4F Wildcat, also tubby

in stature but possessed of a much superior performance. In the hands of a good pilot, the F4F was almost a match for the Japanese fighters. The best approach to dealing with a Zero by the summer of 1942 was to employ two Wildcats against a single Japanese A6M. Moreover, by the time of Midway a series of movements had been created by senior USN pilots, notably Commander Thach, to combat the more agile and seemingly unbeatable Zero. The combination of these movements and 'glue-like' flying would at least give the pilots of the Wildcats a stronger chance for survival than their predecessors of only six months earlier. Unfortunately, not all pilots were briefed in anti-Zero tactics, and many were quite fresh, and the result was heavy losses for the US fighter units at Midway.

By 1940, the dive-bomber was seen by most naval air arms as the principal attack weapon. Like the fighter, this type can trace its origins back to World War I. It is commonly believed that the US Navy and Marine Corps pioneered the dive-bombing technique during the latter half of the 1920s, but in fact the Royal Flying Corps had started to employ angled dives on to targets in order to increase their accuracy during the second half of World War I. These were generally shallow dives, but not always. What the USN and USMC did was to increase the angle of the dive as a regular technique and then adopt it as a standard attack profile. During the 1930s this form of bombing was explored by other air arms, notably

The Aichi D3A Val was a superlative dive-bomber at the outbreak of the Pacific War, but by Midway it was starting to show its age, particularly against better-trained and aggressive US pilots.

'The first months of the Pacific War were a disaster for U.S. forces, and Marine Air felt the brunt of it. First were the appalling losses at Pearl Harbor. What followed at Wake Island and then at Midway painted an even darker picture. Americans were going into combat in inferior aircraft against a foe whose aviators were seasoned veterans. Of the twenty-five fighters that intercepted the incoming raid at Midway, fifteen were blown out of the sky, and only two remained serviceable after the fight. The bombers fared little better. What success the air units enjoyed was a matter of intrepidity, not preparedness.' – J. Trotti, *Marine Air: First to Fly* (CA: Presidio Press, 1985)

The Douglas SBD Dauntless was the American 'hero' at the Battle of Midway. This is truly one of the few aircraft that can be classed as a war winner. Only 13 of these aircraft would drop bombs on Nagumo's carriers, but that would be enough to turn the tide of the Pacific War.

those of the Germans, the French and the Japanese. The last had been using aircraft in shallow dives for some time, but during the 1930s they were able to introduce dedicated dive-bombing aircraft. By 1940 the standard Japanese exponent of the art was the Aichi D3A, or 'Val' to the Allies. With a stressed skin but a fixed undercarriage (partly to act as air brakes in the dive), the 'Val' was an extremely accurate and very steady dive platform. Its bomb load, however, was lighter than that of other dive-bombers: it was hugely influenced by earlier German machines, and accuracy seemed to be more important than bomb capacity. The D3A would provide the backbone to the carrier dive-bombing squadrons for the Japanese for much of the Pacific War, accounting for more

Allied ships sunk than any other aircraft in World War II as a whole.

The US equivalent to the 'Val' was the Douglas SBD Dauntless. It was a rugged machine, designed by the legendary Ed Heinemann. Its range was shorter than that of the 'Val', but it carried a heavier bomb load – an important factor in the Battle of Midway. In aerial combat it was slightly inferior to the 'Val', and, at first, Dauntless air crews were mostly novices, with very few veterans aboard. The Dauntless did not represent modern technology at the time of Midway – its development was a somewhat lengthy process – and a replacement, the Helldiver, was already lined up. It came about as a result of a US Navy requirement for a dive-bomber during the 1930s, and during the war was employed not just by the USN, USMC and USAAF but other Allied air arms as well. In total, nearly 6,000 would be built. Unsurprisingly, it accounted for more Japanese ships sunk than any other Allied aircraft during the Pacific War. Perhaps more importantly, the SBD ('slow but deadly') Dauntless is one of the few aircraft in aviation history that can genuinely claim to have changed the outcome not just of a single battle but of a war, on account of its successes at Midway. However, it did suffer heavy losses during the battle: over 40 of the carrier-based SBDs were lost and most of the Midway SBD dive-bomber force was destroyed as well, with eight shot down and a further five very badly damaged.

Torpedo-bombers were the world's first anti-shipping aircraft, and, like fighters and dive-bombers, were developed during World War I. Indeed, the Japanese had attempted to employ air-launched torpedoes against German and Austrian shipping during the Anglo-Japanese assault on Tsingtao, in China, in November 1914. However, the generally accepted first successful torpedo sinking caused by an aircraft occurred during August 1915, when a number of Turkish vessels were disabled and sunk by the Royal Naval Air Service in the Dardanelles campaign. By 1918, both ship-based and land-based torpedo-bombers were a feature of almost all naval air arms. The aerial torpedo, although smaller than submarine- and ship-launched equivalents, was increasingly feared by surface ships, and by the end of World War I had already achieved a number of successes, prompting the development of various counters during the inter-war period.

The **Dauntless SBDs** would become the heroes of the hour during the battle. They would by a combination of luck and deduction by their squadron commanders, locate the IJN carriers and through heavy anti-aircraft fire ultimately plant 13 bombs onto the flight decks of the enemy ships. This would demonstrate the dive-bomber as the most effective aerial ship killer of the USN. However, following Midway it was recognised by both the USN and USMC that the SBDs were not the frontline equipment needed desperately by their flyers. Even though the dive-bombers were the instruments that stopped the Japanese attack the SBD overall performance was judged to be too poor to be retained as frontline attack bombers. They were seen as practical only for training. Of course, they would, however, be retained in frontline carrier service until 1944, and in land based operations until 1945. But Midway must be seen as their greatest moment.

By the time of Midway the Douglas TBD Devastator was considered an obsolete design. Although flown courageously, the American torpedo-bomber squadrons did not stand a chance against the Japanese Mitsubishi A6M Zeros used for carrier combat air patrol.

The basic World War I design of a biplane with a torpedo and a crew of two or three, flying at 100mph or so, held sway until the late 1930s, when Japan and America began introducing faster, monoplane designs. The Douglas TBD Devastator was procured for the USN, entering service in June 1937, whilst the Nakajima B5N ('Kate') was ordered into production for the IJN in November 1937. The TBD was heralded as not merely the most advanced torpedo-bomber in the world but also the most modern carrier aircraft of its day. Sleek and up-to-date, and with an enclosed cockpit and a retractable undercarriage, it looked positively futuristic, until 1938 when the B5N entered service, which looked even more impressive and was far more capable in terms of speed and range. By the time of Pearl Harbor, the B5N was still the best torpedo bomber in the world.

The D3As and the B5Ns constituted the IJN's carrier-based 'punch', and both were flown by campaign-hardened professionals, creating for the Japanese very expert 'ship-killers' by the time of Midway. The same could not be said of the TBDs. Their first major encounter with the Japanese Navy was during the Battle of the Coral Sea, and, although successful, they suffered casualties and showed themselves to be vulnerable against enemy air defences. Making matters worse was their relatively ineffective torpedo, which compared poorly with the heavier

CARRIER-BASED AIRCRAFT AT MIDWAY (IJN AND USN)	
Mitsubishi A6M 'Zero' **Range:** 1,200 miles (1,900 miles ferry range) **Speed:** 332mph **Armament:** 2 x 7.7mm MG, 2 x 20mm cannon	**Grumman F4F Wildcat** **Range:** 770 miles **Speed:** 318mph **Armament:** 6 x 0.5in MG
Nakajima B5N 'Kate' **Range:** 1,237 miles **Speed:** 235mph **Armament:** 1 x 7.7mm MG, 1,764lb torpedo or bomb load	**Douglas TBD Devastator** **Range:** 716 miles **Speed:** 206mph **Armament:** 2 x 0.5in MG, 1,000lb torpedo
Aichi D3A 'Val' **Range:** 840 miles **Speed:** 180- 267mph **Armament:** 3 x 7.7mm MG, 1 x 550lb and 2 x 132lb bombs	**Douglas SBD Dauntless** **Range:** 1,100 miles **Speed:** 245mph **Armament:** 2 x 0.5in MG, 2 x 0.3in MG, 1 x 1,600lb and 2 x 325lb bombs

and more deadly weapon that equipped the IJN. Even more important was the TBD's limited production numbers. Only 129 were delivered to the USN, as in the late 1930s the Navy was unsure whether torpedo aircraft were even required. However, by 1942 a replacement, the Grumman TBM, was already flying. Six of these new torpedo aircraft would take part at Midway, but they would be operating from the island itself and ultimately have the same physical impact as their older companion – none at all.

Both sides employed floatplanes launched from cruisers for reconnaissance purposes during the war, particularly the Japanese. Of most interest are the Japanese seaplanes of the cruisers and battleships of Nagumo's Striking Force, as they would play a major role during the battle. Aichi E13A ('Jake') seaplanes on the battleship *Haruna* and cruisers *Chikuma* and *Tone*, along with Mitsubishi F1M ('Pete') seaplanes on the battleship *Kirishima*, were employed by Nagumo for prior warning of an approach by the US Fleet. Additionally, a large number of Nakajima A6M2-N ('Rufe') seaplane fighters were aboard the carriers *Chitose* and *Kamikawa Maru* with the invasion force. These could have proved very useful to Nagumo during the battle, and certainly to Yamamoto after the loss of his First Carrier Striking Fleet. The IJN was in the process of introducing dedicated carrier-based reconnaissance assets, giving the fleet very long-range notice of enemy vessels. The Yokosuka (or Kugisho) D4YC ('Jill') was being introduced, and a handful were embarked on *Soryu*, but, strangely, they were not used in the reconnaissance role during the Midway operation. Instead, the seaplanes from the escorting cruisers and B5Ns from *Akagi* were employed for this purpose.

The US had, of course, the Midway air garrison, which had been strengthened by Nimitz as a result of the forewarning by 'Hypo' of Japanese action. It comprised a large number of mixed land-based aircraft and flying boats of the USMC, USAAF and USN.

THE MIDWAY AIR GARRISON	
USAAC/USAAF: Detachment of the Seventh Army Air Force: 4 B-26, 19 B-17E	
USMC: Marine Air Group 22, 2nd Marine Air Wing	
VMSB-241: 16 SBD, 11 SB2U-3 Vindicators	
VMF-221: 20 F2A-3, 7 F4F-3	
Plus 5 'spare' SB2U	
USN: VT-8: 6 TBM	
Patrol Wings 1 and 2: 38 PBY-5/5A Catalina	

F4F Wildcat		**TBM Avenger**	
Range:	770 miles max.	**Range:**	1,130 miles max.
Speed:	318mph max.	**Speed:**	267 mph max.
Armament:	6 x 0.5in MG	**Armament:**	3 x 0.5in MG, 1 x 0.3 in MG, 2,000lb bomb load
F2A Buffalo		**PBY Catalina**	
Range:	965 miles max.	**Range:**	2,545 miles max.
Speed:	321 mph max.	**Speed:**	179 mph max.
Armament:	4 x 0.5in MG	**Armament:**	3 x 0.3in MG, 2 x 0.5in MG, 4,000lb bomb load
SB2U Vindicator			
Range:	1,120 miles max.		
Speed:	243 mph max.		
Armament:	2 x 0.5in MG, 1 x 1,000lb bomb		

Thus, in total, Nimitz and his commanders in theatre had at their disposal over 220 carrier-based aircraft, with a further 120 other combat aircraft on Midway to set against Yamamoto's forces at the start of June. Although this inventory was bigger than Nagumo's, the figures do not take into account the other Japanese air assets around Midway – had they been concentrated. Additionally, the inferior quality of a large number of the American aircraft has to be emphasised, along with their command and control problems. Captain Simard USN (Officer Commanding Midway NAS) fought his own battle, separate from that of Admiral Fletcher and the US carriers, as there were no communications between the two American forces. To make matters worse, Simard's information and recommendations for action originated with his three subordinate air commanders, from the USMC, USN and USAAF, on Midway. The result was poorly co-ordinated and executed attacks. Ironically, their value came with their unco-ordinated attacks, which became important diversionary raids and helped to convince Nagumo that a second strike against Midway was essential. This last factor is worthy of note, as the confusion over whether to neutralise the islands totally or wait for American carriers brought about a turning point in the battle, although the cost was, effectively, the island garrison's entire air assets.

Plane for plane, and air crew for air crew, the IJN possessed the upper hand. In terms of range, speed, battle experience, training and flying time in the air, the Japanese were on the whole superior. There were a number of novice crews amongst Nagumo's carriers, and the shortages of good veteran air crews back in

the home islands of Japan were starting to be seen. The majority of IJN air crews at Midway, however, were knowledgeable and confident of victory. The Americans, on the other hand, were generally inexperienced and flying inferior aircraft, as the after-battle air reports made quite clear. However, the deciding factors in the battle were not simply going to be aircraft performance statistics but the behaviour of the men in their aircraft and, more importantly, the decisions of their commanders before, during, and after the battle.

The Catalina PBY proved itself an exceptional patrol craft. It was a Catalina that located the approaching Japanese warships.

5

THE BATTLE
THE AMBUSHER IS BUSHWACKED

Over the sixty or so years that have elapsed since the Battle of Midway, a degree of controversy has come to exist over what exactly happened during a crucial part of the clash between the Imperial Japanese Navy and the United States Navy during the morning of 4 June. Perhaps more importantly, the question is asked why the Japanese lost a battle they should, in all rights, have won. Most notably, recent interest has centred upon Admiral Nagumo's actions on board *Akagi*, and the IJN's seemingly slow reactions during the early part of the engagement. The Japanese seemed to have been suffering from either over confidence or great lethargy, together with an apparently total lack of urgency on the part of their carrier commanders to strike the US Pacific Fleet once the position of Fletcher's task forces had finally been ascertained. The run-up to the battle is accepted by most commentators, as are the final hours of the engagement, but the morning of the 4th is increasingly shrouded in confusion, theory and counter-theory. In recent years, as a result of new research and increased availability of Japanese sources, a number of historians have offered some new explanations of the events on board the IJN carriers that fateful morning, and these interpretations are increasingly helpful in analysing and explaining why the Japanese lost at Midway and in clarifying what really went wrong for Yamamoto, Nagumo and the Combined Fleet.

By 25 May, Rochefort's 'Hypo' team of code-breakers and cryptanalysts at Pearl Harbor had uncovered and agreed the timings, strengths and targets for Yamamoto's Combined Fleet. This clarified and confirmed for Nimitz and his staff the major areas of concern and planning for the next ten days. Indeed, from 22 May Nimitz had already begun to send all available defensive equipment, aircraft, guns and tools to Midway in order to bolster its defences and give the US forces there at least a fighting chance. The US Marines, commanded by Colonel Shannon USMC, defending the beaches of Midway, had assured Nimitz that, given the right equipment and enough of it, they would be able to repulse a Japanese amphibious assault. They had inflicted heavy losses on the Japanese in earlier encounters, for example that at Wake, so the Marines possessed more than a degree of confidence, even if this opinion was not necessarily shared by 'mainland' American military observers.

To achieve any hope of a successful defence, the Marines and Nimitz had to be continually vigilant. The vital information from the code-breakers would have to be supported by a constant watch of the surrounding waters in order to help fulfil the Marines' beliefs. Consequently, Nimitz despatched, and the commanders on Midway chose continually to employ, a large number of Navy PBY flying boats from Patrol Wings One and Two for long-range reconnaissance around the waters of the islands. The PBYs would fly out to distances of over 700 miles and give the Midway defenders early warning of approaching IJN forces, aided in the last resort by the radar station on the islands. The PBY aerial reconnaissance missions were stepped up in early May, and from the 21st they were part of Midway's alert status. However, in June the number of sorties was drastically increased, and this development would prove crucial in the battle. All of this was fortunate for the Americans, as from 26 May Yamamoto and the Combined Fleet set sail from Ominato and Hashirajima in Japan and from Saipan and Guam for their attacks against the Aleutians and Midway.

Nimitz's second objective was to get his three available carriers, including the badly damaged *Yorktown*, replenished and sent on their way to Midway as quickly as possible. Halsey's Task Force 16, with *Hornet* and *Enterprise*, was back in Hawaii by 26 May, having voyaged from the Western Pacific and the South-East Asian theatre. Fletcher and the USS *Yorktown* arrived a day later, on the 27th. Halsey's return had been slower than some would have expected. His departure from South-East Asia had been deliberately delayed by Nimitz to allow Japanese

Of the three US carriers present at the Battle of Midway, USS *Yorktown* must have been the most unlikely. Almost sunk at Coral Sea and in desperate need of a long refit, repair work was none the less turned around at Pearl Harbor in three days, enabling her to perform a crucial role in the battle that stopped the Japanese.

forces to witness TF.16 and its movements 'in-theatre'. This would give the impression that a good proportion of America's limited carrier power was nowhere near the IJN and the Midway Islands.

However, convincing the IJN of his ship movements seemed to be one of Nimitz's lesser problems. Of more importance to him was the state of Fletcher's TF.17. *Yorktown* had suffered badly at the hands of Japanese air crews during the Battle of the Coral Sea at the start of May, and yet the critically battered carrier was readied for action in less than three days. This was the result of a herculean effort by the American dockyard workers and support teams in Pearl Harbor, readying the ship for combat (it was estimated at the time that repairs to Fletcher's carrier would normally have taken at least three months). It was *Yorktown*'s complete fitness for battle that enabled her to play a crucial role in the engagement. *Yorktown*'s extra flight deck and air group together with inaccurate IJN intelligence concerning the positions of TF.17 and TF.16 would all greatly aid the Americans.

By 29 May, Nimitz, again by courtesy of his code-breakers ('Hypo' and Melbourne), knew that the second Japanese invasion force, heading towards the

---

Had either the Japanese submarines managed to get on station early, or the two US Task Forces been running late, the outcome of the battle could have been vastly different. The US Navy's greatest asset, surprise, would have been lost. The IJN would have known for certain that the Americans were aware of its plan, and Yamamoto would have realised that Nimitz was taking action to stop the Japanese seizure of Midway. Consequently, he could have altered his plan (unlikely) or, having now been informed of the US presence, he could have concentrated on dealing with the US carriers and left Midway as a mopping up operation for later (more probable). Additionally, the Japanese submarines could have carried out their other mission, which was to attack and whittle down any US forces heading westwards from Hawaii. If even just one US carrier been either sunk or simply disabled by Yamamoto's submarines, then the course of the battle would, again, have undeniably been altered.

In fact, so important were the Japanese submarines that Nimitz had to neutralise them. The USN partly deterred and partly delayed the IJN submarines by placing ships and aircraft along their route. This was a ploy that was also used to deter any long-range flights by, and refuellings for, Japan's large flying boats. These were supposed to carry out reconnaissance for the Combined Fleet, which included making close approaches to Pearl Harbor. Unfortunately, this was one mission that they could not complete, leaving a void in Japan's intelligence concerning the US and its carriers in South-East Asia and forcing the IJN to rely on earlier sightings. This is what makes Nimitz's earlier order to Halsey to loiter in-theatre important.

Aleutians, was scheduled to attack the northern American territories prior to the Midway assault. Crucially, however, he knew that this was only a diversion. 'Hypo' also knew that the IJN forces had been spilt up into seemingly myriad groups, thus failing to concentrate, and offering the US Navy a glimmer of hope in the forthcoming battle. However, by the end of May Nimitz was also fully aware that before Midway was invaded it would be attacked and 'softened-up' by Admiral Nagumo's 1st Carrier Striking Force, which consisted of at least four carriers, supported by a number of battleships and cruisers. Thus numbers still seemed against the US admiral, even though he did have the benefit of knowing the approximate bearing of the enemy carriers. Rochefort and 'Hypo' were convinced that Nagumo would approach Midway from the north-west whilst Yamamoto's Main Body and invasion force would come from the west and south-west, respectively. This division of forces seemed inappropriate from the American point of view, but they welcomed it nonetheless.

Despite their huge advantage of foreknowledge, the odds against the Americans were still worryingly stacked against them. From the Aleutians in the north down to Midway in the central Pacific, the IJN would be deploying eight

Little could these airmen in their Devastators of VT-6 (shown here on USS *Enterprise*) know that they would be wiped out in their valiant and seemingly fruitless attacks against Nagumo. But these ponderous torpedo bombers proved the key to unlocking the decisive moment during the battle.

fleet and light aircraft carriers, eleven battleships and dozens upon dozens of cruisers and destroyers – in total, more than 150 ships. As we know, to counter this huge Japanese battle order the US Pacific Fleet could muster only the barest of assets. To hold Midway and essentially stay in the war in the Pacific for the remainder of 1942, Nimitz could commit to the forthcoming battle at Midway no more than three carriers, eight cruisers and fourteen destroyers, with a further five cruisers and thirteen destroyers sent north (TF.8) under Admiral Theobald to engage and harass the Japanese Aleutians forces.

In addition to the formidable IJN surface fleet, twelve Japanese submarines, detached to form an arc-shaped patrol line west of Pearl Harbor, were supposed to locate and identify the US Pacific Fleet were it to sail west from its base in response to any attack on Midway. Due to Rochefort's timely decoding work, however, *Enterprise* and *Hornet* sailed from Pearl Harbor on 28 May, *Yorktown* getting under way the following day. Thus the watching Japanese submarines formed their patrolling arc a day too late to sight the three American carriers on their way to a rendezvous at 'Point Luck', a non-existent speck in the Pacific some 300 miles north-east of the Midway Islands. By 3 June, *Yorktown*, *Hornet* and *Enterprise* were ready and lying in ambush, with the Japanese having no idea they were there.

The Japanese, however, were not totally blind to US actions in the run-up to Midway. The IJN intelligence services were aware of increased radio traffic and

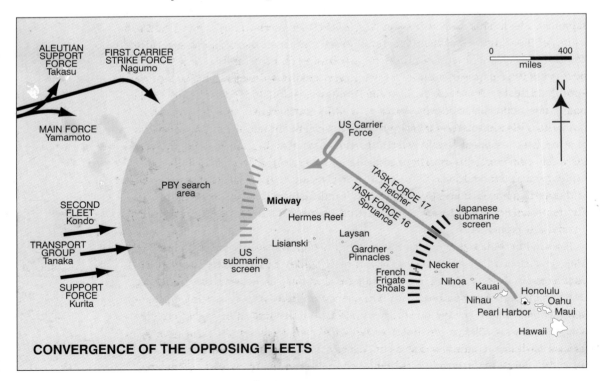

CONVERGENCE OF THE OPPOSING FLEETS

activity in and around Midway and Pearl Harbor, although they could not pinpoint the reasons behind this. For this very eventuality, Task Force 16, on leaving Hawaii on the morning of 28 May, had in fact set a course taking it north of the islands. This would take it away from any Japanese submarines and give the impression of a possible Aleutians mission were the US carriers to be spotted. However, soon it turned its course towards Midway, and by 1 June it was in position north-east of Midway. By 2 June, Fletcher's Task Force 17 had of course rendezvoused with Spruance's ships at 'Point Luck' – a thoughtful and most fortuitous name. Neither of the task forces should have worried about alerting the IJN, as they were not detected. Although the two forces were brought together, they were not combined into a single tactical unit. Instead, Fletcher operated ten miles to the north-west of Spruance, acting, in theory, as the vanguard of the US force and its reconnaissance element. If any Japanese presence were to be sighted, Spruance would act as the striking force, moving up to engage the Japanese carriers. Whilst Task Force 17 would continue to act as the reconnaissance force and a reserve of aircraft and ships for Spruance, Admiral Fletcher, on board *Yorktown*, was in overall command of both task forces.

Fletcher's plan was to rely on the Midway-based PBYs to carry out the majority of the reconnaissance work against the Japanese. The range of the PBY would facilitate early warning but, more importantly, should at the same time enable his own carriers to remain undetected. He would thus hold back until the air searches from Midway had identified the most important element in the Japanese Fleet. This of course was Nagumo's fleet carriers, and, upon notification of these, he would then set about doing what he could to halt them. If he could simply cripple them, besides inflicting lasting damage on the IJN he would be forcing the Japanese to think twice about attacking Midway in the face of the combined strike element based on the American islands and his carriers. This policy has been described by some as a little conservative and defeatist, but, given the odds seemingly stacked against him and the limited number of carriers at America's disposal, there was little else that Fletcher could do. He was definitely not in a position to fight a sea battle on equal terms with the Japanese, trading carrier for carrier, nor aircraft for aircraft, and he knew this. Indeed, Midway might well become a last-ditch stand against the IJN onslaught, and Fletcher was not going to sacrifice some of the last US carriers without a result against the Japanese.

Having left their home ports in Japan and the Marianas Islands at the end of May, Yamamoto's Fleet made its way, mostly under radio silence, across the Pacific to its destiny. By 1 June, as they headed east, they were encountering treacherous Pacific weather, with fog, rain and high winds causing station-keeping problems – problems compounded by the fact that there were so many ships in so many different groups. On the other hand, however, the poor weather as least gave the Japanese a degree of secrecy, something they had been lacking up to this point, as the conditions blanketed their ships from possible US patrols.

The Mitsubishi A6M Zero, the most famous of all Japanese aircraft. The Zero's agility, seeming invincibility and ubiquity at the start of the war belied the fact that these fighters were few in number and suffered from a number of deficiencies. That said, the Zero still managed to dominate much of the war in the air until 1943.

3 June

By 3 June the bulk of the Combined Fleet was moving into position for its roles in the attack on Midway. In the north, the Japanese Aleutians forces were already in position and were beginning their onslaught, which got under way at 0800 as aircraft from the two carriers of the Northern Striking Force, *Junyo* and *Ryujo*, attacked US forces in Dutch Harbor. Nimitz was quickly informed of the attacks, but he was not going to alter his plans and come to the aid of his compatriots in the north, barring the despatch of Admiral Theobald's limited Task Force 8. They were going to have to survive with what they had. The attack on the Aleutians convinced all within the American fleet off Midway who were aware of 'Hypo' intelligence that the code-breakers were more than merely on the right tracks: the hunches and guesswork that had characterised a number of the opinions directed to Rochefort and his companions were now replaced by the cold, hard reality of confirmation, and the more terrifying prospect of almost immediate battle with the heart of the IJN. The Japanese fleet was on its way to Midway. First, however, the Aleutians campaign was to begin. It was a struggle that was to last far longer than either side could have guessed, and one that saw quite devastating consequences for the IJN when an almost intact A6M

Zero was captured by the Americans, enabling them to discover the weaknesses of this 'invincible' aircraft.

More poor weather and events (or the lack of them) around the Aleutians soon forced the realisation on to Yamamoto and his admirals in the north that any easy, big successes were not to be had in this theatre. The IJN's first carrier strike against US targets was diluted when the aircraft from *Junyo* failed to find Dutch Harbor, whilst *Ryujo*'s were too few to inflict serious damage. Another strike in the morning also failed to find the target, owing to very poor visibility. The omens did not appear good for the IJN.

The First Carrier Striking Force reputedly sailed to its destiny in a land-attack formation rather than the IJN's battle formation. This may have had implications for its defensive firepower, particularly from anti-aircraft artillery (AAA) on board the ships of the fleet. The light cruiser *Nagara* headed Nagumo's force. Behind the cruiser came the two battleships, *Haruna* and *Kirishima*, with the four carriers either side of the battleships. The heavy cruisers, *Chikuma* and *Tone*, were then placed on the flanks, along with a number of escorting destroyers. This has struck many commentators as being far from the optimum disposition for ships requiring defence against heavy air attack, particularly regarding the battleships with their strong AAA.

However, although the Aleutians attack was a diversion, both sides knew it (though the Japanese did not realise that the Americans knew it), and, more importantly, both sides knew where the main show was about to take place.

By noon on the 3rd, Midway's PBYs, on near-continuous patrol around Midway, had finally picked up IJN forces heading towards the tiny atoll, the aircraft reporting a sighting of the 'Japanese Main Body'. However, Pearl Harbor was later able to inform Fletcher that this was the invasion fleet and not Nagumo's carriers. On Midway, however, the air units were readied for a sortie against the hostile ships. By midday the shadowing PBYs had located all of the IJN ships approaching from the south-west, including Kondo's Main Body, Kurita's support force and the actual invasion force of Tanaka. With this information, Midway launched nine of its B-17s from 1225, its only bombers with sufficient range to hit the IJN fleets reportedly 600 miles and more away. At 1640 the B-17s dropped their bombs, but they missed their targets. Later in the evening, three PBYs managed to find the IJN ships and launch a night-time strike. They managed to damage a transport but failed to force it out of line. It was fairly obvious to Yamamoto that his plan, and his force, had been discovered earlier than anticipated, yet he maintained course whilst simultaneously failing to share this information with the rest of his units, notably Nagumo. Perhaps of more importance was the fact that these strikes against the invasion fleet demonstrated that Midway was not just alerted to the presence of the Japanese but was also prepared for them.

The Japanese invasion force might well be under attack, but very little could be done by the US to locate Nagumo's Striking Fleet. The foul weather that the IJN carriers had encountered crossing the Pacific was still lingering around the waters north-west of Midway, shielding Nagumo's fleet from observation.

Nonetheless, preparations continued on board the American carriers to find the Japanese strike force in the morning of the 4th. On Nagumo's ships, the Japanese crews also carried out last-minute checks for their strike against Midway, but they seemed blissfully unaware that the US Pacific Fleet carriers were sitting to the north-east of Midway preparing to strike at them.

4 June

Dawn on the 4th saw the two fleets begin to launch their aircraft. Fletcher sent off his reconnaissance aircraft as ten SBD Dauntlesses were despatched to locate Nagumo's carriers. Spruance's flyers were readied for action, whilst, on Midway, Navy PBYs were airborne, adding to Fletcher's SBDs. The island's B-17s were preparing to take off on another bombing mission against the Japanese, while the remaining torpedo-bombers, dive-bombers and fighters were waiting to launch at a moment's notice. Their readiness was as much to do with avoiding annihilation on deck as being ready to strike at the IJN once the Midway radar had warned them of any approaching Japanese aircraft.

By 0430, Nagumo's four carriers – *Akagi*, *Kaga*, *Soryu* and *Hiryu* – were ready to launch their softening-up strike against Midway's defences. The first strike would consist of 36 A6M Zeros for fighter cover and ground strafing, along with 36 B5N 'Kate' level bombers (their torpedoes were discarded in favour of bombs on this occasion) and 36 D3A 'Val' dive-bombers. Nagumo held back 108 of his available strike aircraft, arming them with torpedoes and armour-piercing bombs for an attack against any possible American warships in the area. Such a possibility, however, was considered very unlikely. Nagumo had not been informed of any American shipping movements, and was therefore under the impression that the US carriers – those few left after the sinkings in the Coral Sea – were still either in South-East Asia or at Pearl Harbor. He had not received any negative information concerning Hawaii; in fact, he had received no information at all. Therefore, he concluded, all was well. However, he kept back half of his air group, armed for the anti-shipping role, for any unexpected eventuality. His prudence was sound and expected. Furthermore, besides acting on strategic intelligence received from Yamamoto and Japan, he decided to generate his own tactical kind, ordering air searches by scout planes from his carriers, *Akagi* and *Kaga*, and from the cruisers *Chikuma* and *Tone*. Unfortunately, and very crucially, there was a technical problem with the catapult aboard the cruiser *Tone*, which delayed the launch of her scout aircraft for half an hour (until 0500). What seemed an unimportant delay at the time has been seen by many since as a fateful occurrence, critical to the whole of the First Carrier Striking Force and, potentially, an incident of crucial importance to the course of the battle.

Reduced to its barest and least-contested form, the traditional view of the battle on 4 June runs as follows. PBYs from Midway sighted Nagumo's carriers (0530) and the incoming strike (0540). All available strike aircraft on Midway were then launched (0600 onwards) to attack the Japanese carriers and escape Japanese bombing. The latter aim was successful (even if the former was not), with the result that none of the US aircraft was caught on the ground when the Japanese air strike hit Midway (0630–0730). The leader of the strike, Tomonaga, radioed back to Nagumo (0700) stating that a second strike was necessary. No sooner had Nagumo ordered his reserve aircraft to be rearmed with bombs rather than anti-shipping weapons for a second strike than *Tone*'s scout plane sighted Fletcher's cruiser and destroyer screen (0728). However, it took another hour before Nagumo was informed that the American force included at least one carrier. Traditionally, the view of the battle has it that Nagumo was caught by indecision and a lack of information, resulting in a series of delayed and confused orders for the air crews and deck crews.

Nagumo was held indecisively for some time between two courses of action. He could either launch his second-strike aircraft, or he could land his returning first strike aircraft and delay the launch of the second wave. Nagumo finally chose to recover his returning aircraft, accepting all the risks associated with the decision. Crucially, by the time all the aircraft that had taken part in the attack against Midway had returned to their carriers, had refuelled and had begun to be rearmed with anti-shipping weapons, it was at least 0917. At this point Nagumo turned his carrier force north-east to close the American force, but it

Admiral Spruance's launch of his aircraft from *Enterprise* (pictured here) and her sister ship *Hornet* was the crucial offensive move that caught the Japanese. Had Spruance waited, the US Fleet would have borne the brunt of Nagumo's planes *en masse*.

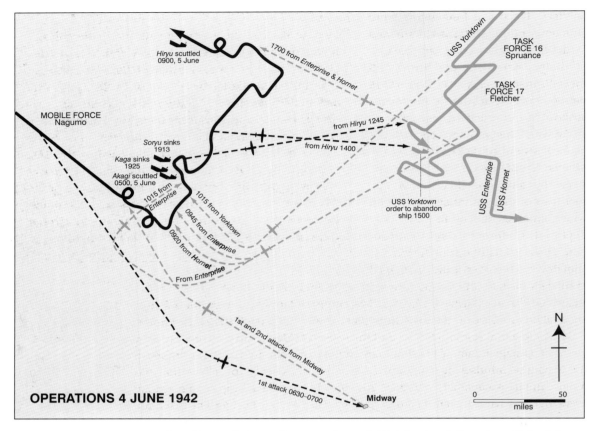

Hiryu scuttled
0900, 5 June

MOBILE FORCE
Nagumo

Soryu sinks
1913

Kaga sinks
1925

Akagi scuttled
0500, 5 June

1015 from Enterprise

1015 from Yorktown

0945 from Enterprise

0920 from Hornet

From Enterprise

1700 from Enterprise & Hornet

from Hiryu 1245

from Hiryu 1400

USS Yorktown

TASK FORCE 16
Spruance

TASK FORCE 17
Fletcher

USS Yorktown
order to abandon
ship 1500

USS Enterprise

USS Hornet

1st and 2nd attacks from Midway

1st attack 0630–0700

Midway

OPERATIONS 4 JUNE 1942

N

0   50
miles

was already too late as Spruance's and Fletcher's strike aircraft had been launched and were airborne, en route to the Japanese carriers.

By 0630, an hour after the first sighting of Nagumo's carriers had been reported to Fletcher, *Enterprise* and *Hornet* began launching their aircraft. *Yorktown* remained behind to recover her search aircraft. Spruance, on the advice of Halsey's Chief of Staff, Captain Miles Browning, had taken the gamble of attacking at extreme range while Nagumo was still committed to the Midway attack. Spruance launched 98 TBD Devastator torpedo-bombers and SBD Dauntless dive-bombers, along with 20 Wildcat fighters. *Yorktown* launched its aircraft ninety minutes later, from 0830 onwards. However, the US launch failed to create the required attack formation involving all three types of aircraft. Devastator torpedo-bombers and Dauntless dive-bombers were supposed to attack simultaneously while being escorted by Wildcat fighters, which would punch a hole through the Japanese combat air patrol (CAP). Unfortunately, many of the squadrons became separated, although *Yorktown*'s F4Fs did manage to stay with their TBDs, albeit with little success. Most of the US torpedo-bomber pilots went in without fighter cover and, relatively inexperienced, paid a heavy price for the brave attacks they made on the Japanese carriers. Thirty-five Devastators were shot down out of a total of 41 launched by the three squadrons taking part.

Vitally, however, the three US torpedo attacks between 0918 and 1015 delayed the launching of Nagumo's strike at the American carrier force – a strike which had already been delayed by no fewer than five attacks by the Midway-based aircraft. Of these, one strike by four B-26 Marauders had seen two of their number shot down, whilst another raid by the six newly deployed Grumman TBF torpedo-bombers saw all but one of the aircraft shot down. The sole survivor managed to make it back to Midway but was critically damaged and crash-landed on the island. Of the 16 Marine Dauntless dive-bombers launched from the islands, eight failed to return, and one of those that did was riddled with 179 bullet holes.

Most of the literature dealing with the battle concentrates, naturally enough, on the IJN and USN aviators on board the carriers rather than on the Midway-based aircraft, but the latter were crucial in the run-up to, and during, the battle. However, the mixture of Army Air Force, Navy and Marine air units was a nightmare in terms of command and control. Moreover, most of the aircraft were not suited to combat against the IJN, although the pilots and crews of the garrison aircraft displayed great bravery and tenacity in the face of the far more experienced enemy crews and, at times, ferocious AAA. That said, the Midway-based aircraft were unable to achieve any hits on 4 or 5 June.

Thus the initial carrier attacks, and those from Midway, were unsuccessful in terms of damage inflicted, but they were important inasmuch as they reinforced the Japanese mindset of confidence. They led the enemy to believe that the American attack capability was poor and also that Japanese ships could readily evade damage from the air. From 0700, Nagumo's carrier fleet was attacked for some 90 minutes by more than 130 aircraft from Midway, none of which managed to land a hit – and at a very heavy price to the air garrison in terms of losses and damage.

As mentioned above, the problem for Nagumo and the IJN was what to do. The admiral had aircraft returning to his carriers from the first strike on Midway, and there were aircraft on his decks that were fitted with a combination of land-attack and anti-shipping weapons following his order to rearm the second Midway strike with weapons for use against the US carriers. If, as some of his subordinates were urging, he launched his 'mixed' second strike, most of the attack aircraft would be flying without cover from Zero fighters and with the wrong type of ordnance. If he waited, Nagumo would have to send the aircraft on deck down to the hangar, land the returning aircraft, then finish rearming and re-spot the second strike for launch. This would be a time-consuming option, and one that would bring the US carrier force ever closer, though probably not close enough for the US to launch a strike in the time available. The IJN knew – even if they slightly underestimated – the ranges of the US aircraft. They also knew that their machines had a far greater range than the US strike planes. Nagumo took the risk and ordered the second strike below and the landing of the Tomonaga's Midway strike force. Japanese CAP would be maintained but it would be hard pressed (as demonstrated by the figures for *Akagi* below) owing to the persistent attacks by the Midway-based US aircraft and the TBDs from the carriers. A constant flow of Zero aircraft on to and from the Japanese decks was required to maintain a steady presence above the IJN force. The problem was how to maintain the CAP. The Japanese fighter pilots were simply expending so much ammunition because of the many US attacks that they were having difficulty keeping a fully armed fighter screen in the air.

The continual movement of Zeros from just the flight deck of *Akagi* indicates the problem facing Nagumo. As the US carrier-borne torpedo aircraft arrived over the IJN fleet, there were some 50 A6M Zeros on CAP.

At 1020, having now beaten off eight American attacks without having taken a single hit, Nagumo's carriers turned into the wind to launch their aircraft, intent on delivering the death blow to the US 'flat-tops'. Precisely at this moment,

The Douglas SBD Dauntless was under-powered, had a short range and was vunerable, but it sank more Japanese ship tonnage than any other aircraft.

Akagi CAP (Combat Air Patrol) List, 4 June

0445: Following the launch of the Midway strike force at 0430, the first CAP is launched (3 A6Ms)

0543: Three more A6Ms launched

0655: Three more A6Ms launched

0659: Three A6Ms recovered

0710: Five more A6Ms launched

0720: One A6M recovered

0726: One A6M recovered

0736: Three A6Ms recovered

0750: Two A6Ms recovered

0808: Three A6Ms launched

0832: Four A6Ms launched

0910: One A6M recovered

0932: Five A6Ms launched

0945: Three A6Ms launched

0951: Two A6Ms recovered

1010: Three A6Ms recovered

undetected because of the Japanese lack of radar and with their CAPs either on the flight decks rearming and refuelling or in the air finishing off the low-flying US torpedo-bombers, the Dauntless dive-bombers from *Enterprise* and *Hornet* arrived over head. Nagumo's carriers could not have been more vulnerable.

The IJN's great vulnerability is explained, in the traditional view of the battle, by the decks of their carriers being packed with aircraft and covered with petrol bowsers and hoses, together with piles of bombs left lying after the abandoned second strike against Midway. Less than five minutes later, three of Nagumo's carriers, *Akagi*, *Kaga* and *Soryu*, were blazing wrecks. Only *Hiryu* was left undamaged to carry on the fight. Nagumo's flagship, *Akagi*, was hit by two bombs which resulted in uncontrollable fires and a series of secondary explosions. *Kaga* was hit by four bombs that produced fires and induced internal explosions, whilst *Soryu*, the first of the three to be struck, was hit by three bombs exploding amongst her parked aircraft and penetrating into her hangar, causing fire from stem to stern. The battle had been turned in some five minutes – and, perhaps more importantly, by fewer than a dozen bombs.

However, *Hiryu* was still afloat, her fighting spirit very much intact. At 1054, in an effort to swing the battle and avenge her sister carriers, she launched her aircraft, D3A 'Val' dive-bombers, together with a Zero escort. These were the first Japanese aircraft to be launched against the American carriers that day, but the IJN aircraft caught only *Yorktown*. The strike seemed accurate and appeared to the Japanese air crews to have been very successful, but in fact it resulted only in the temporary crippling of Fletcher's ship, which received three bomb hits shortly after noon. The fires on board *Yorktown* were put out, and steam was raised again in just two hours. However, a second strike from *Hiryu*, this time with B5N 'Kate' torpedo aircraft and a small Zero escort at 1445, put *Yorktown* out of action again, this time permanently. Some of the Japanese were now convinced that they had disabled two US carriers.

This belief was shattered when the unscathed *Enterprise* and *Hornet* launched a second American strike against the last of Nagumo's operational 'flat-

USS *Yorktown* in the midst of battle attempting to ward off attacking Japanese aircraft. The US carrier would be struck by two waves of attacking Japanese, but this sacrifice was essential as during the battle the Japanese aviators believed they had sunk both US carriers present. They were quickly re-educated when aircraft launched from the *Enterprise* and *Hornet* attacked and hit the *Hiryu*.

The Dauntless dive-bombers had initially failed to find Nagumo's fleet, but then Lieutenant-Commander Clarence Wade McClusky, commanding *Enterprise*'s SBDs, working on hunches and with a disregard for his fuel reserves, spotted a lone IJN destroyer, *Arahi*. In front of this ship he spied three of Nagumo's carriers. *Hiryu* was not spotted as she remained hidden under the ever-changing cloud cover present over the Japanese ships for much of the battle. McClusky and his Dauntless flyers divided into two groups and aimed for *Kaga* and *Soryu*. Simultaneously, *Yorktown*'s SBDs arrived overhead and started to dive on Nagumo's flagship, *Akagi*. Much of the Japanese CAP was still far from its proper patrol altitude, which meant that it was unable to engage the SBDs as they approached their dives, though were able to attack them at lower levels once the American aircraft had finished their runs. As a result, eighteen of McClusky's group of 33 Dauntlesses were never to return to their carrier.

tops'. In this instance the strike consisted only of Dauntless dive-bombers as the ships were denuded of torpedo aircraft following to the loss of the TBDs earlier that day. This second American strike found and wrecked *Hiryu* shortly after 1700. The Japanese carrier was attacked by 24 SBDs and was hit by four bombs on her forward flight deck, starting unstoppable fires. Amazingly, the Japanese carrier was able to maintain speed, and it looked as though there was a chance of survival for the ship. However, the fires started by the bomb hits gradually spread, trapping and killing many of the *Hiryu*'s crew members below decks. Eventually she stopped. Nagumo's last carrier burned all night, and sank the following morning at 0910. The IJN's First Striking Fleet had been destroyed and the Battle of Midway was effectively over. The Japanese had lost.

The foregoing summarises the oft-recounted, accepted course of events of 4 June 1942, and this interpretation has been repeated since the end of World War II in a myriad works dealing with the battle. However, it does not tell the whole story, nor does it really explain why the Japanese lost. How was it that just over a dozen bombs effectively destroyed the bulk of the IJN offensive power and altered the course of the Pacific War? Does the traditional view adequately tell us how this really happened? The answer is yes, only if one is willing to accept the basic chain of events – that the US dive-bombers arrived over the decks of the carriers devoid of CAP, and with the carrier decks strewn with aircraft refuelling

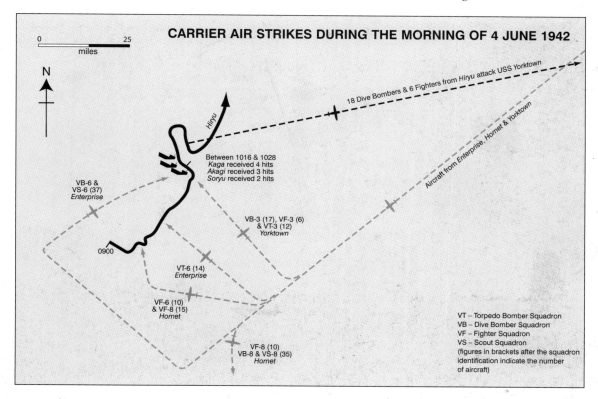

CARRIER AIR STRIKES DURING THE MORNING OF 4 JUNE 1942

0 — 25
miles

N

18 Dive Bombers & 6 Fighters from *Hiryu* attack USS Yorktown

Aircraft from *Enterprise*, *Hornet* & *Yorktown*

Hiryu

Between 1016 & 1028
Kaga received 4 hits
Akagi received 3 hits
Soryu received 2 hits

VB-6 &
VS-6 (37)
Enterprise

VB-3 (17), VF-3 (6)
& VT-3 (12)
Yorktown

0900

VT-6 (14)
Enterprise

VF-6 (10)
& VF-8 (15)
Hornet

VF-8 (10)
VB-8 & VS-8 (35)
Hornet

VT – Torpedo Bomber Squadron
VB – Dive Bomber Squadron
VF – Fighter Squadron
VS – Scout Squadron
(figures in brackets after the squadron
identification indicate the number
of aircraft)

Right: A Japanese
bomber scores a
direct hit on the
carrier USS *Yorktown*
during the Battle of
Midway. *Yorktown*
faced two waves of
Japanese aircraft,
both from the IJN
carrier *Hiryu*. The first
wave was a strike of
Val dive-bombers
with Zero escort,
while the second was
a strike of Kate
torpedo bombers,
again with Zero
escort. Both scored
hits on the US carrier.

and rearming and with ordnance piling up, and then bombed the Japanese carriers. Admiral Nagumo's short-comings, bad luck, unfortunate timing and poor Japanese procedure, together with confusion, order and counter-order, lost the commander of the First Striking Fleet his ships and therefore the battle. But is this really true?

The scenario traditionally described – that of a confused Nagumo, a tardy reconnaissance aircraft and a lethargic response by the IJN carrier fleet – cannot be taken for granted. We must ask ourselves a number of questions, and these have increasingly been asked. Why did it take Nagumo almost an hour from the time he received the information that US ships were present north-east of Midway (0728) to the time his rearming procedure was altered? Why did it take so long to rearm? Why did it take so long to ready his strike against the US carriers? And why did the IJN carriers fall victim so quickly to the US Dauntless dive-bombers after so many earlier attacks had failed and been beaten off? We do not have, and probably never will have, a complete picture of what went on aboard the Japanese carriers, and some intelligent conjecture – supported by new sources of information and unclouded by a dogmatic allegiance to the accepted, often unsupportable versions of the battle – is therefore required.

It would seem that *Tone*'s scout plane was less than tardy in its reporting. Initially it reported the presence only of US cruisers and smaller escorts, because that is all it initially saw, and in overcast conditions. In fact, these ships were probably the cruiser screen for the US carriers. The larger warships were not sighted because they had moved off in order to launch their aircraft. The Japanese aircraft would have been keen to transmit the position of any US ships, to give as much early warning as possible to the IJN fleet. The transmitted information was encrypted, and sending and receiving it was therefore a time-consuming process. It was followed up by further transmissions which highlighted the position of US carriers as and when they came into view – and, again, this information was subject to delays because of the encryption and deciphering process. The last point is important, as it seems likely that Nagumo received the information concerning the presence of US ships, including carriers, after 0800 rather than the traditionally accepted time of 0730. A number of

Hiryu afire. She was the only successful Japanese carrier during the Midway engagement. She managed to strike USS *Yorktown* twice before she herself succumbed to the remnants of the US Navy's carrier striking force from *Enterprise* and *Hornet*.

Japanese officers claiming to have been present when Nagumo received the report from *Tone*'s scout plane support this interpretation, amongst them Genda. Why did it take so long? The logical answer is because the aircraft first relayed its information to its 'mother ship', *Tone*, and the cruiser would then have to pass it to the flagship, *Akagi*, where finally it would have to be passed to Nagumo for his consideration.

If this is true, then it throws the whole of the accepted chain of events into doubt. It alters all of the opinions concerning the Japanese reaction and the 'delay' in rearming the aircraft, presenting us with a picture not of lethargy or overconfidence on the part of the IJN carrier commanders on the morning of 4 June but one of hurried activity and working to a known schedule. The IJN armourers and fitters knew how long it would take to rearm entire squadrons of aircraft, but in this instance they were being forced to rearm whilst recovering aircraft from the Midway strike, recovering and re-launching Zeros of the

CAP and then re-spotting their anti-carrier strike for launch – a tall order, and one to be met in some two hours as Nagumo wanted to launch before 1030.

Amazingly, they almost succeeded. A few extra minutes would have seen the IJN air crews take off, and the battle would have hung in the balance as the carrier fleets of both sides had their pilots airborne simultaneously. Thus, increasingly, the battle took the form of a struggle to be decided by the winner of a race against time rather than by luck or ill-judgement. It would seem that Nagumo was a victim of the situation in which he found himself rather than the villain of the events. It could also be argued that, had *Tone* launched her scout plane on time, it might well have missed the American ships completely and even less warning time would have been received by the Japanese admiral.

That said, Nagumo was undeniably decreasing the flexibility of his ships when he initially, at 0715, ordered the rearming of his torpedo-equipped reserve aircraft for a second bombing strike against Midway. Furthermore, there are still questions concerning the vulnerability of Japanese carriers and the ease with which they succumbed to the handful of bombs dropped on to their decks by the US dive-bombers. Another question is whether or not the IJN carriers really were crowded with aircraft as the SBDs struck. Some American pilots were convinced that there were very few aircraft on the Japanese decks, just a handful of rearming Zeros. Either way, the vulnerability of carriers to dive-bombers was well known. The IJN First Striking Fleet had despatched HMS *Hermes* in April in a powerful dive-bombing attack, but perhaps a more useful lesson would have been that taught by HMS *Illustrious* in the Mediter-ranean, which suffered at the hands of German Ju-87 Stuka dive-bomber crews. The British armoured carrier was hit by six bombs and survived thanks only to her armoured deck and hangar, and her close proximity to Malta, where she was bombed again but survived. Neither the Japanese nor the American carriers were heavily armoured like their British counterparts, and they were therefore that much more vulnerable to bombing. It was hardly surprising that the IJN carriers succumbed once hit, even though they succumbed to somewhat inefficient bombs.

5 June

Taking stock on the night of 4/5 June, Yamamoto was forced to accept that it was Nagumo's carriers that had lost the race to strike first against the US carriers and had, as a consequence, met the annihilation intended for the US Pacific Fleet. Though still possessing crushing naval superiority, Yamamoto could only use it if the Americans advanced within range of the Japanese Navy's guns and torpedoes. He ordered a combining of the Main Body and Kondo's force, and, later, the remnants of Nagumo's fleet, in an attempt to join battle *en masse* with the Americans. He was also still determined that Midway would fall, and ordered a series of night bombardments against the islands by cruisers and submarines. Nagumo claimed that he could not join the growing force in time, and as a result

Yamamoto appointed Kondo in his place. It would seem that the C-in-C of the Combined Fleet had had enough of Nagumo's 'timidity'. The two Aleutians carriers, *Junyo* and *Ryujo*, were also ordered south by Yamamoto – Operation 'AL' was temporarily suspended – to join the newly combining Japanese force around Midway.

The reorganisation was all to no avail. Admiral Spruance, who had taken tactical command when Fletcher abandoned *Yorktown* at 1500 on the 4th, avoided any hasty action and held back. In fact, TF.16 began moving east, in order to lessen the chances of a night engagement with the Japanese, which the US knew would see their own numerical inferiority in surface ships crushed by the IJN force. It is concerning this decision that some commentators have made the case that the Americans were both wise and fortunate to have had Spruance in charge of TF.16 and not Halsey. A Halsey-led TF.16, it is argued, could, as a result of this commander's well-known aggressive fighting spirit and confidence, well have seen the night action the superior IJN were seeking, and this would have finally dealt the decisive Japanese blow against the US Navy from which the latter would have been unable to recover until late 1943. On the other hand, Yamamoto knew that he could only proceed with the Midway attack by exposing his fleet to unopposed air strikes during daylight. This, to him, would have been an acceptable risk only if he knew how many US carriers and how many aircraft on Midway were confronting him. If the Midway garrison had been destroyed along with the bulk of the air groups on the carriers, then the risk to his fleet was minimal; if, on the other hand, he faced a large aerial armada (which seemed unlikely but could not be ruled out), it was potentially very serious. Yamamoto contemplated for some time, but finally he decided against the continuation of the operation. He cancelled the occupation of Midway at 0255 on the 5th, ordering the Combined Fleet to turn back from the small atoll, and reopened the Aleutians campaign.

This was not the end of the suffering of the Imperial Japanese Navy, as at 0215 the US submarine *Tambor* was sighted by some of Kondo's cruisers, resulting in a collision between the cruisers *Mogami* and *Mikuma*. As the IJN left the scene of its disaster it was forced to administer the *coup de grâce* to its wrecked carriers. At 0455 *Akagi* was sunk by Japanese torpedoes, and shortly afterwards (0500) *Hiryu* was torpedoed by the Japanese destroyer *Makigumo*, sinking finally at 0910. As daylight returned to the waters around Midway, the withdrawing IJN found themselves chased and attacked by the remaining airworthy Dauntless, Vindicator and B-17 bombers from *Enterprise* and *Hornet* and from Midway. The interests of these remaining US aircraft were the two damaged cruisers (0810–0850), of which *Mikuma* was sunk.

Yamamoto's decision not to continue in the attempt to seize Midway is quite incredible and one of the most important decisions of the Pacific War. Had he persisted, he would have met the US fleet, its remaining air elements and possibly surface units. Not only did he possess more ships than the US Navy, his aircraft also outnumbered the Americans' machines on and around Midway at this particular time. He was still supported by his two seaplane carriers, *Chitose* and *Kamikawa*, and by his two small carriers, *Hosho* and *Zuiho*. These were carrying aircraft that would have been useful in continued offensive and defensive operations against Midway and the US fleet, and equal in number to the remaining US machines. Some were arguably inferior – the 'Rufe' seaplanes, A5M 'Claudes' and B5N1 'Kates' – but there were A6Ms and B5N2s on board *Zuiho*.

Had the IJN continued to Midway, landed, and seized the islands, the US would have been forced to retake them. This they would not have been able to achieve for some time, enabling Yamamoto to have built up Midway's defenders and bring his other fleet carriers in to play whilst simultaneously extending the Japanese defensive perimeter, and thereby extending the war. This is a huge 'What if?', but a very apposite one.

6 and 7 June

Thus Yamamoto's fleet was already in full retreat to the west when the last-minute American strike by a combination of aircraft from *Enterprise*, *Hornet* and

The Japanese cruiser *Mikuma* reduced to a blazing wreck by US Navy aircraft.

the remaining bombers on Midway caught the lagging cruisers *Mikuma* and *Mogami*. In fact, the US air crews carried out a number of aerial attacks against IJN surface ships, from battleships to destroyers. They were unable to make any impact, a combination of heavy anti-aircraft fire and well-controlled ships denying the US any further victories. In return, the IJN denied the Americans the chance of saving *Yorktown*; the shooting had not quite finished. On 6 June, shortly after dawn, the crippled US carrier was torpedoed twice by the Japanese submarine *I-168*, which also sank the destroyer *Hammann* standing by. The valiant US carrier finally sank at first light on 7 June, ending the Battle of Midway. The battle for the Aleutians, however, would continue into 1943.

Described by some historians as a 'theatre of military frustration', the Aleutians saw a long, attritional struggle by the Japanese and Americans, albeit a struggle not in the same league as that for Guadalcanal. The IJN had trumpeted the seizing of Attu and Kiska islands and were therefore forced to defend them. The US was determined to eject the Japanese forces from American territory as a matter of pride, and also because the territory was required for possible use as a staging point for forces destined for Russia. The islands are bleak, fog-shrouded and weather-beaten, and are notable for only one naval engagement of any scale – the battle of the Komandorski Islands on 26 March 1943, in which an inferior US force comprising one heavy and one light cruiser, together with four destroyers, gave battle to a Japanese force commanded by Admiral Hosogaya and consisting of two heavy and two light cruisers together with four escorting destroyers. The resulting action saw the Japanese disengage, even though they had succeeded in inflicting more damage than they received (the Americans almost losing their heavy cruiser). This engagement effectively ended any hopes Japan might have harboured of retaining long-term control of the islands. Gradually US forces, together with their Canadian allies, increased their force levels in and around the Aleutians, and by late July 1943 they were ready to push the Japanese out of the Aleutians altogether by retaking Kiska, having already taken control of Attu. Following a large amphibious assault, the US forces found that the 5,000-strong Japanese garrison on Kiska had withdrawn under the cover of the typically foul Aleutians weather. American territory – and honour – had been regained.

Why Did the Japanese Lose?

Recent opinions about the Battle of Midway are perhaps more credible than the 'traditional' accounts. One has to be suspicious of those who continually thrust forward a simple 'list of reasons for the defeat of the Japanese', particularly concerning the concept of 'victory disease'. This theory answers a number of questions, but it also strikes many as an excuse. The four carriers, the air crews and the admirals that day represented the heart of the most efficient carrier striking fleet the world had seen – and it was a combat-proven force. It had devastated Pearl Harbor and cleared South-East Asia, the Bay of Bengal and much of the Indian Ocean. When the IJN's destiny went unfulfilled at Midway on 4 June, the Japanese as much as anyone else had to offer explanations. They did so with half-truths and by identifying scapegoats, and they were aided and abetted in this cover-up by US commentators, the US Navy and subsequent historians. One fact generally ignored in the quest to explain the Japanese defeat that day is simply that the US Navy was superior to its enemy, and this deserves examination.

When the Imperial Japanese and US Navies met off Midway, their respective strengths would have led one to suppose that the Japanese would win the engagement. However, the Americans turned the battle, and the course of events for the rest of 1942, to their favour. 'How were the Americans able to win at Midway?' has become one of the most commonly asked questions ever since. Merely stating that the US Navy was better on the day, while obviously true, requires a fuller explanation. Very little occurs as the result of a single factor, either in war or peace. Events are usually the result of a series of factors, sometimes apparently unrelated. Midway was no different.

By June 1942 the Japanese had the most professional and best-equipped aviators (and, in theory, the finest aircraft carriers) in the world. The Royal Navy had been fighting since 1939 and possessed many skilled veterans, but on the whole it flew poor aircraft from too few carriers. The Americans had only been

Crew and airmen of *Yorktown* tread carefully on the listing deck of the doomed carrier.

in the war six months and had received bloody nose after bloody nose at the hands of the Japanese. The IJN seemed to possess the best pilots, together with the best aircraft, and only the Battle of the Coral Sea had been able to give some comfort to the USN. However, that comfort came at a price – the loss of one of its biggest carriers, *Lexington*, and some of her valuable air crews and aircraft. It was the Japanese, with experience since 1937 of fighting in the air and of numerous carrier operations who were the true professionals. However, there were not enough of them, and at Midway newer Japanese pilots, less well trained than their predecessors and lacking in experience, were appearing in the squadrons aboard Nagumo's carriers. On the whole, however, the IJN should have carried the day, simply through sheer weight of numbers. Why, then, did Yamamoto fail to achieve his 'decisive battle' at Midway? Numbers, equipment and skill levels were, after all, in his favour.

What is not often mentioned is how close things really were. The battle could easily have resulted in the Japanese victory that Yamamoto believed destiny would give him. Had Nagumo launched earlier, or Spruance later, the outcome would probably have been reversed. As it was, the destruction wrought on the flight decks and in the hangars of the four Japanese carriers came about from just over a dozen bombs. This is a surprisingly small amount of ordnance,

The battered *Yorktown* lies abandoned after the second successful Japanese air strike.

considering how many aircraft and how many munitions were launched against Nagumo's carrier fleet that day. It can therefore be argued that 'a baker's dozen' of bombs decided the course of the Pacific War – a tiny expenditure deciding the course of a momentous struggle.

That said, and in all fairness, there were some inherent underlying factors that were working against the Japanese whilst simultaneously aiding the Americans. Leadership is a crucial factor in all engagements. Unfortunately, the IJN leadership failed. All, from those in high command to the leaders on the scene, were guilty of failing the men they commanded and the nation they served. Tokyo was at fault, for allowing the plan to stand as it was. Yamamoto failed, as it was he who forced the plan, whilst his subordinate commanders failed to shape the rigidity and complexity of his strategy. However, as Commander-in-Chief of the Combined Fleet, Admiral Yamamoto must bear the heaviest burden of responsibility. He appeared to be driven more by the need to defend Japan and the Emperor (and by revenge for the Doolittle raid) and less by the military logic of actually destroying the US Fleet. The result was a planning stage and implementation phases that were both blinkered and poorly executed. The force of his personality drove through what many believed to be an ill-conceived concept. Moreover, his leadership, and certainly his motivation for the battle, failed at perhaps the crucial point. The evening of the 4th, when there was still a chance to seize Midway and compensate the IJN for the day's losses, went unfulfilled. Yamamoto failed to maintain the aim of the operation, and he failed to maintain the morale of his command. These are major deficiencies in any military operation.

The make-up and execution of the plan to seize Midway and destroy the US Pacific Fleet also bears a heavy responsibility for the IJN losses in June. It is the lack of concentration of forces on the part of the Japanese that is often stated to be the primary failing among many. Over six decades later it is still difficult to understand the logic behind a number of the decisions which led to the splitting up of the Pacific's most powerful naval force. Schoolchildren of today who have run wargames of Midway do not make the same cardinal error that was made in 1942, ensuring that when they take on the role of the Japanese admiral they appear at the appointed destination with everything – together! However, it must be remembered that Yamamoto was not solely responsible for the complicated plan, nor for the minutiae within the decisions to divert: others had a large hand in its eventual format. However, as Commander of the Combined Fleet, he should have been aware of the error of splitting his units and failing to give maximum concentration to his forces.

The lack of simplicity within the plan, once finally formulated, was also a major failing. There is no denying that it was overly infused with assumptions, timings and pointless diversions. The IJN planners failed to keep things simple. They possessed vastly superior forces compared to Nimitz, but the IJN failed to use this superiority of numbers and *matériel* to its advantage. Yamamoto's supposed background in naval aviation and belief in the carrier leaves one wondering why he divided his carrier forces, and why he did not employ the battleships of the Main Body to escort them. Why did he have so many different groups, and what was he doing so far behind Nagumo?

As well as suffering because of an overly complicated plan that lacked cohesion and logic, the IJN was the victim of failed security. Personnel were unable to transmit anything in secrecy, and consequently the Navy lost the element of surprise. Even allowing for the failure to concentrate ships, the IJN could still have crushed the enemy at Midway, but the plan's failings combined with its lack of security meant that Yamamoto's 'decisive battle' was doomed. The ability of the Americans to read so many of the IJN's codes and ciphers meant that the element of surprise – so often vital to a successful operation – was lacking. It undermined most, if not all, of the Japanese assumptions regarding American dispositions and intentions, with the result that the Japanese carriers became the victims rather than Nimitz's ships.

Overconfidence is often cited as another reason for IJN's failure at Midway. Certainly, most Japanese were confident of victory during the preparatory stages of Operations 'MI' and 'AL', but many commentators have suggested that this overconfidence, or 'victory disease' as some have termed it, was an important factor in the Japanese defeat. Commanders and their air crews within the IJN were naturally confident, having gained so many victories, but not perhaps as confident as many would have us believe. By June 1942 the carriers had had six months of near-constant activity. Any confidence the men possessed was tempered by the knowledge that the 'originals' who were left were tiring, and that the Americans' fighting spirit was improving with every engagement. Coral Sea demonstrated that, when pre-positioned and co-ordinated, the US Navy could stop and damage Japanese forces. The Tokyo Raid in April had also shown the Americans to be ingenious and far from lacking in courage. By June 1942 elements within the IJN were already realising that the early victories were not going to be repeated. 'Victory disease' did not permeate the Combined Fleet. It was apparent only amongst certain personnel and ships within the IJN in June, and, rather than being a major factor for failure, it can only be seen as being of some significance in explaining the losses.

The gathering and flow of information are also major factors in the successful prosecution of war. Unfortunately, not enough information had been gathered by the Japanese concerning US ship movements – not for a want of trying, but because the Americans' knowledge of Japanese intentions enabled Nimitz to block enemy reconnaissance-gathering missions. Information that did reach Yamamoto was not passed forward to his commanders, particularly Nagumo on board *Akagi*. It seems that Yamamoto believed that any information he was receiving would naturally be reaching Nagumo as well, but this is a critically important, and unwise, assumption upon which to build and run an offensive. The result was that Nagumo was effectively kept in the dark.

A picture of indecision and confusion is often painted of Nagumo on board his carrier. He indeed failed to seize the moment, but this is again, perhaps, an over-emphasised view, partly to save Yamamoto from criticism and to demonstrate that it was one of his group commanders who was at fault and not the Commander-in-Chief or the whole of the Imperial Navy. However, Nagumo could only make his decisions as a result of the flow of information into his carrier. He had already demonstrated early in the conflict that he made decisions based on solid information and acted accordingly. When information failed to materialise – and some of it was deliberately withheld – then there must be some sympathy for a commander who has to make decisions based either on false information or on none at all. It could well be when he finally was given concrete information – for example, the reports from *Tone* after 0800 rather than around 0730 – then he acted as best he could.

Offensive spirit in battle is also crucial to success. This may not have been evident in Yamamoto's actions during the night of 4/5 June, but the seeds had

An unfamiliar picture of Japanese prisoners being landed on Midway Island after the battle.

The Grumman F4F Wildcat was the backbone of the US Navy's carrier-based fighter force. Wildcats also served on garrison duties with USMC flyers, as at Midway, along with Brewster F2A Buffaloes. The Wildcat had to be flown by a skilled aviator to stand a chance of survival (let alone success) against the Japanese Zero in the summer of 1942.

been sown for the Japanese long before. Perhaps the two best examples are the IJN air crews' failure to wear parachutes during their combat missions, as a result of which a number of good pilots and other air crew were needlessly lost, and the imbalance of aircraft types aboard the Japanese carriers. The offensive aircraft – the D3As and B5Ns – vastly outnumbered the mostly defensive A6Ms. There were simply too few Zeros to allow successful CAP and offensive fighter escorts to be flown for Nagumo. After Midway, the Japanese changed the balance of their carrier air groups to reflect a slightly stronger fighter presence. For example, *Shokaku* and *Zuikaku* both carried more A6Ms (27 rather than 21) at the expense of attack aircraft, as a direct result of their experience. Some carriers almost dispensed with attack aircraft altogether, going to the opposite extreme and suggesting that a defensive mindset may have been initiated within the IJN. Certainly, the demands placed on the Japanese CAP at Midway were too much for Nagumo's carriers to cope with, and holes were bound to appear as the Americans continued their aerial onslaught. The US attacks may have been poorly co-ordinated, but in the end this did not matter as the SBDs found huge holes through which they were able to strike.

Certain technological deficiencies were also apparent on the Japanese side, most notably the lack of radar. The overstretching of Nagumo's fighters during the battle could have been partially avoided had the IJN ships possessed radar, but unfortunately the IJN was only just beginning to introduce it on board their ships at the time of Midway. Two ships in Yamamoto's Combined Fleet during the battle did indeed possess radar, but both were battleships in Yamamoto's Main Body and thus of no value to Nagumo. The lack of radar meant that the IJN were forced to rely solely on aerial reconnaissance and last-minute look-outs on board the ships of the fleet. Neither proved to be successful. The possession of radar would have given the IJN time to organise, time to regroup into battle formation and time to marshal its CAP properly. The months following Midway saw a drive in the IJN, somewhat belated, to improve the situation amongst its carriers, but it would not be until the spring of 1944 that the first Japanese carrier equipped with radar, *Taiho*, would enter service.

The design of the Japanese ships, and their deployment, must be seen as factors contributing to the IJN's defeat. The quality of construction and strength of the Japanese carriers seemed inferior to that of their US counterparts, although this point is still debated today. Less contentious was the Japanese defensive armament – too few anti-aircraft guns, combined with a general failure of the escorting vessels to shield the IJN carriers. Nagumo's escorting battleships and cruisers seemed very capable of defending themselves from air attack but did not extend these capabilities to their important charges. Of more concern was the standard of damage control on board the carriers. This was influenced by the construction of the ships and the training of the crew, and perhaps it is here that we can detect a hint of complacency. A successful navy, destined to win a glorious decisive battle, may relax its training in damage-control procedures on board its ships. At no real point from 1937 until the Battle of the Coral Sea were the IJN challenged in any substantial way, and the time that elapsed between Coral Sea and Midway was too short for any major lessons to be implemented. The result was what can be considered inappropriate and insufficient damage control on board Nagumo's carriers.

Their losses at Midway apart, the failings of the Japanese need to be put into a wider context of US strengths. Having spent much of the previous six months 'on the back foot', and despite being vastly outnumbered at Midway, the US forces on the whole performed well, and nothing should be taken away from their achievement. American leadership can be held up as an excellent example of command. It was well informed, willing to delegate and ready to take risks, both in Hawaii and off Midway. The US commanders were far more flexible than their adversaries, both at the point of contact and back at headquarters, and seemed far more successful in appointing appropriate people for the tasks in hand. From Nimitz down through his task force commanders and the squadron commanders, the US leadership was often inspired but, more importantly, correct in its beliefs and actions.

The leaders were aided by a number of technical advantages. Radar was crucial to the US forces, particularly in the defence of the US carriers and of Midway itself. Far more damage could have been achieved by the IJN air crews had less warning time been given to American aircraft. The US aircraft that survived, due to this extra warning time, were able to play a crucial part in the battle, forcing Nagumo to order a second Midway attack and to enable *Yorktown* to survive its first strike and force *Hiryu* to strike again. *Yorktown* demonstrated other successful US areas of superiority, for example the quality of construction of their ships and the damage control on board. Granted the IJN carriers were struck by numerous bombs (at least three per ship), but *Yorktown* was hit equally heavily but at first survived, compelling the Japanese to renew their efforts to sink her.

It is undeniable that US aircraft and weapons systems were generally inferior to those of the Japanese, but the fighting spirit of the American airmen – again, both those from Midway and those from the carriers – was instrumental in achieving the US victory that day. The tenacity of the US pilots equalled that of the IJN pilots and perhaps sometimes bettered it, although US pilots reported that IJN fighter pilots would fly into the fire of their own AAA to shoot down incoming US aircraft, knowing full well the weaknesses of their A6M Zeros.

The US forces were able to create strategic luck around Midway. If fortune were favouring the brave on 4 June, then it was the Americans who were the braver and more fortunate. The loss of the TBD squadrons, although in itself a terrible tragedy and a Japanese tactical victory, allowed the US dive-bombers virtually free rein over the IJN 'flat-tops'. Thus a tactical failure on the part of the US air groups facilitated a strategic success in the Battle of Midway and the loss of the Japanese carriers.

However, possibly the most important factors of all were the psychological factors that existed during the battle – the states of mind not just of the American commanders but of everyone on the ships and on Midway. Essentially, the IJN was not fighting for its life, whereas the US Pacific Fleet was most certainly fighting both for its very existence and, possibly, for that of the United States. Perhaps therein lies the reason why there were so many differences between the two navies on that fateful day in June 1942. Ironically, two years after Midway, at the Battle of the Philippine Sea, the IJN would find itself in the same position that Nimitz and his small fleet had found themselves during their crucial battle. The Japanese, however, would have neither the leadership nor the material where-withal to turn their battle, nor to alter the outcome of the war in their favour. After Midway, that outcome was never in doubt.

6
AFTERMATH
IMPLICATIONS OF THE JAPANESE DEFEAT

The Battle of Midway came to a close with the sinking of *Yorktown*, which slipped below the waves at around 0600 on the morning of 7 June. Four days later, on the 11th, the Tokyo press announced a great Japanese naval victory at Midway. Nothing, of course, could have been further from the truth. So concerned and embarrassed was the IJN over the losses at Midway that it attempted to keep the real figures secret. At first, only one carrier was said to have been lost, but the IJN was correct when it spoke of a decisive battle. What was omitted was the fact that it was a decisive victory for the US Navy, bringing the enemy closer to the shores of the home islands and not further away as intended.

Midway was indeed the turning point in the Pacific War. The IJN would go on to build and convert another twenty carriers. It would produce over 10,000 A6M Zero aircraft and another 10,000 carrier-based machines of other types. Thousands of naval aviators would be trained, together with thousands more engineers, aircraft maintainers and support crews, but these figures would pale into insignificance when compared to the US production figures for World War II. In aircraft carriers alone, the Americans produced more than five times the Japanese output. Never again would the IJN have such overwhelming superiority over the USN as it did in June 1942. The Japanese would continue to win battles into 1943, but they were only buying time, and they were buying it with the remnants of the fine fleet and air arm with which they had started the Pacific War. The Battle of Midway was supposed to stop the United States from intervening in the Japanese exploitation of South-East Asia, and to protect the Japanese home islands from attack by US aircraft. In these aims, Yamamoto and the IJN failed miserably.

Moreover, not only had the IJN lost a very significant part of its most potent weapon – four of its carriers – but it had given more than just a glimmer of hope to the US. Admiral Nimitz and his task forces had not merely stopped Nagumo's carriers; they had destroyed them. Even in the light of the positive yet mixed results from the Battle of the Coral Sea in May, many Americans believed that the war against Japan would be hard, costly and long, and that there was a possibility that it might not go to America's liking. The pessimists were right in a sense, but Midway undeniably shortened the war by removing some of Japan's best assets just six months after the outbreak of hostilities.

The ensuing battles around Guadalcanal from August 1942 until February 1943 saw the IJN lose even more carriers and valuable crewmen, resulting in the realisation by spring 1943 that the IJN was unable to mount another large-scale carrier offensive, although the US Navy was also reeling: *Hornet* and *Wasp* were both lost off Guadalcanal, leaving *Enterprise* as the sole operational US carrier

In some ways the Grumman F6F Hellcat was a legacy of the Japanese failure at Midway and in the Aleutians. The Hellcat would come to dominate air combat against Japanese naval aviators from late 1943, shooting down more Japanese aircraft than any other US aircraft.

for a time. So desperate was the USN for carriers that it 'borrowed' a British carrier, HMS *Victorious*, during 1943 to make up the shortfall. The difference between Japan's difficulties and those of the US, however, was that the American losses would be made good very quickly – and in terms not only of quantity but also of quality. The new 33,000-ton *Essex* class carriers that entered service towards the end of 1943 carried more aircraft, and more potent aircraft, than either the *Yorktown* class at Midway or the Japanese carriers.

After Midway, the writing was very much on the wall for Yamamoto and the Imperial Japanese Navy. However, they did not give up. The IJN's code of honour, its devotion to the Emperor and its determination to defend the home islands and their way of life would ensure that the Americans would have to fight to force the Japanese from every square yard of conquered territory. The fight would be a bloody and brutal one, and the battle of Midway was just a small taste of what was to come.

The battles for Guadalcanal, which would see a number of significant naval engagements (in particular off the Eastern Solomons and at Santa Cruz) were brutal and attritional, for both man and machine. In fact, the struggle for Guadalcanal might have gone either way. As it was, the US was able to halt any further territorial gain for Japan and repulse the Imperial Japanese forces, whilst simultaneously blunting much of the IJN's remaining offensive capability. The Japanese were finally evicted from their foothold on American soil, the Aleutian Islands, in 1943, but, again, not before heavy losses were incurred on both sides. As mentioned earlier, perhaps the most serious setback for the Japanese was the loss of an essentially intact A6M Zero. Taken back to mainland America, the aircraft was repaired and test-flown, and the myth of the invincible Zero, which even in early 1943 was still proving to be more than a handful to the US pilots, was blown away. Its weaknesses were identified: American designers were amazed at what the Japanese had created – a lightweight gun platform, with no strength for taking punishment nor any protection for the pilot. With this information, the US Navy was able to hone its tactics and introduce counters to the IJN air menace. This, together with the introduction into service of new American aircraft such as the Grumman F6F Hellcat and Chance Vought F4U Corsair, gave the USN the required ascendancy in the skies over the Pacific. Hence the vital discovery in the Aleutians was one more by-product of the IJN's defeat at the Battle of Midway.

Another by-product was the belief by the US that the sooner Yamamoto were removed from the Second World War the better. He may have been the architect behind the disaster of Midway, but he was a strong and unifying character amongst the Japanese hierarchy and people. He had been behind the Pearl Harbor strike, he had shaped the IJN carrier force into the best in the world in 1941, and he had come close to winning a series of successful battles – Midway, Santa Cruz and the Eastern Solomons. Essentially, Yamamoto was too dangerous. Thus, on 18 April 1943, following continued successful USN code-breaking, an aircraft in which Yamamoto was travelling was ambushed. His small fighter escort was shot down, as was Yamamoto's plane, killing him and perhaps ending any chance of delaying the Americans in the Pacific. He was replaced by a series of Japanese admirals that were simply not up to the job.

By the end of June 1943 the US Navy was ready to launch its counterstroke against the Japanese in Operation 'Cartwheel', an advance up the Solomon Islands chain. This was the beginning of the famous US 'island-hopping' campaign against Japanese-held islands in the south-west Pacific. The process would continue into 1944 and 1945, culminating in massed carrier strikes against the Japanese home islands and the eventual defeat of the Japanese Empire. Before this could occur, however, the US Navy had to move across the Pacific, ever closer to Japan, and destroy the IJN.

The Japanese Navy, even without Yamamoto, was not going to allow the US easy access. They decided to engage and attempt to defeat Nimitz's forces in the

Marianas island chain. This was doubly important for Japan. Not only would it blunt the USN's offensive, but it would also stop the Americans from basing heavy bombers on islands within range of Japan. The resulting Battle of the Philippine Sea in June 1944 (or 'Marianas Turkey Shoot', as it became known to US pilots), failed to live up to Japanese expectations. Once more an over-complicated IJN plan, requiring exact timing and co-operation from a series of forces including ground-based aircraft, failed to deliver the decisive victory. The results were frighteningly bad. The bulk of the remaining experienced carrier air crews, and some 300 Japanese aircraft – ten times the number of US losses – were lost to larger numbers of better-piloted US machines during the battle. What had been left of the IJN carrier fleet after Midway and Guadalcanal in terms of its air crews was destroyed. The remaining carriers – and the IJN possessed these ships in numbers, with more under construction – increasingly found themselves without air groups, while the IJN's training pipeline, shortened and overstretched, began to collapse. The air crews reaching the front line were mere shadows of the personnel who served during the first six months of the Pacific War. The IJN's failure to rotate its crews condemned their best men to death.

Worse was to come. The Battle of Leyte Gulf in October 1944 was yet another Japanese attempt to win a decisive victory over the rampaging American fleets, and again it became a victim of over-complication. Here the Japanese carrier fleet, with minimal numbers of aircraft aboard, was squandered as a decoy to lure Halsey's Fast Carrier Force away from the US invasion fleet sitting off the coast of the Philippines. The ploy worked, but the ensuing ambush of the US amphibious forces failed, with disastrous losses for the IJN surface fleet, and at the end of the battle the ocean-going Japanese Navy had effectively ceased to exist. With their ships gone, the IJN turned to perhaps the most deadly and certainly the most terrifying of all weapons employed at sea in World War II – the *kamikaze* aircraft.

First employed in numbers during the Battle of Leyte Gulf, the *kamikaze* soon became a standard, and to some degree successful, weapon of attack for Japan. Its origins lay with the Japanese military code of honour, but its recent ancestry was the Battle of Midway. The losses sustained by the IJN carriers in the first six months of the war, culminating in Midway and compounded by the brutal struggle around Guadalcanal, where a squadron's survival could be measured in weeks and possibly only days, sounded the death knell for the IJN's air force. The four years required to train an inter-war pilot could not be sustained in wartime. The production of new carrier-borne aircraft also fell well short of requirements: the Japanese industrial base simply could not cope, either with demand or with speedy innovation. Consequently, Japan found herself with a great many below-average pilots and an even larger number of generally inferior aircraft. By using one of the poorly trained pilots and a single aircraft on a one-way mission, the Japanese Navy (and very soon the Army Air Force) might see the destruction of a destroyer or the crippling of a carrier, helping to delay the US advance. The air crews would be helping to save Japan and her way of life, and would be dying in honour of the Emperor and rewarded by promotion and a journey to the Yasakuni shrine, where they would meet their fellow *kamikazes* and be revered for all time. It was their duty, and there was no shortage of volunteers.

The success of the *kamikaze* was startling. For example, from April to June 1945, as the Allies invaded Okinawa, suicide aircraft alone managed to kill 5,000 Allied sailors and wound another 5,000. In many respects this was massed modern naval warfare, as the IJN unleashed thousands of missiles against the attacking fleets – missiles with human targeting computers. Crucially, the United States and her Allies did not know how many *kamikazes* there were and, perhaps more importantly, how long their navies could withstand sustained aerial attack. The war had to be brought to a more rapid conclusion.

The combination of carrier strikes, USAAF long-range bombing, the destruction of the Japanese merchant marine and the declaration of war by the Soviet Union, together with the dropping of the atomic bombs on Hiroshima and Nagasaki in August 1945, finally forced the surrender of Imperial Japan. The Battle of Midway played a significant role in this final victory as the halting of its advance and the destruction of a crucial part of its carrier fleet placed the IJN in a position of equality with the US in 1942, and, as many Japanese realised, this position could only deteriorate. The loss of carriers, air crews, aircraft and support staff could perhaps have been made good and in many ways was, but by then it was too late. The gigantic US war engine was running, and it was only a matter of time before it would crush the enemy.

Things might have been different. The inevitable outcome could have been delayed. Perhaps total defeat, or at least the impact of massed bombing of the homeland, could have been deflected or softened had the IJN and Yamamoto won at Midway. In that event, the Japanese would have held the initiative, and had the ascendancy in the Pacific until at least the end of 1943, when the first of the new *Essex* class carriers began to enter service. The IJN would have moved from a position of dominance over the USN in June 1942 to one of overwhelming superiority. This would have forced the US Government to refocus its war aims, and shift the emphasis from the Atlantic theatre to the Pacific. Ships and equipment destined for the Mediterranean, Great Britain and perhaps even the Soviet Union would have had to have been brought into play in the Pacific. All of this would have undermined and altered the path of victory in Europe.

The importance of the Midway engagement and the defeat of the IJN there had ramifications far outstripping the geographical significance of two small islands in the middle of the Pacific Ocean. Midway was not just a turning point in Pacific War; it was a turning point in World War II as a whole. It was a point that the IJN had itself created. The Japanese Navy might just have as easily explored another avenue – a move into the Indian Ocean, further action against Australia or simply a consolidation of Japanese holdings in South-East Asia.

The Grumman TBM Avenger was the replacement for the Devastator but had only been produced in relatively small numbers by the time of Midway. Unfortunately for the US Navy, only six were available for the battle, flying from Midway itself. They did not fare well, five being shot down. Later in the war the Avenger would become a vital component in the US Navy's counter-offensive across the Pacific.

However, driven by Yamamoto and his combined thirst for revenge for the Tokyo bombings and the neutralisation of the US Pacific Fleet, the IJN found itself staring at defeat in June 1942. As events turned out, the Imperial Navy found that it was neither mentally nor physically prepared for the Midway operation as conceived in Yamamoto's mind. Nimitz and his commanders were, physically, as prepared as they possibly could be; more importantly, they were mentally equipped for the battle ahead. The IJN was not fighting for its life, whereas the US Pacific Fleet was fighting both for its own existence and for that of the United States. Therein lies the explanation of the American victory.

1921–22
Nov–Feb Washington Naval
Conference places restrictions on
capital ships and aircraft carriers.
Feb Anglo-Japanese Naval Alliance
ends.

1930
April London Naval Conference
places further restrictions on naval
construction.

1931 Japan annexes Manchuria.

1932 Japan establishes the puppet
state of Manchukuo.

1933
24 Feb Japan leaves the League of
Nations following censure of its
actions in Manchuria.

1934
19 Dec Japan refuses to be bound by
the Washington Naval Treaty.

1935
15 Jan Japan declares Washington
Naval Treaty to be void after 31 Dec.
1936.
15 April Douglas XTBD-1 first flown.
This will later enter USN service as
the Devastator, the mainstay of the
USN's carrier torpedo-bomber
squadrons at Midway.

1936
15 Jan Japan leaves London Naval
Conference.
25 March Great Britain, the United

States and France sign the London
Naval Treaty.

1937
Jan Nakajima B5N Shinzan
(Mountain Recess, or 'Kate') Navy
Type 97 carrier attack bomber first
flown.
7 July 'China Incident': Japanese
forces attack Chinese troops.
13 Aug Fighting breaks out between
Japanese and Chinese troops in
Shanghai. War escalates.
25 Aug Japanese Navy blockades
Chinese ports.
2 Sep Grumman XF4F-2 first flown
and later enters service with USN and
USMC as the Wildcat.
Dec Brewster XF2A-1 first flown. Will
later enter service with the USN and
USMC as the Buffalo. Will also be
used by British, Australian and Dutch
forces against Japan.
13 Dec USS *Panay* sunk whilst
convoying three oil tankers on the
Yangtse.

1938
Jan Aichi D3A Navy Type 99 Carrier
Bomber ('Val') is first flown.
11 July Japanese-Russian border
clashes. Japanese defeated.

1939
1 April Mitsubishi A6M Reisen or
Zero-sen (Zero, 'Hamp' and 'Zeke')
Type 0 Carrier fighter is first flown.
May–Aug Japanese-Russian border
clashes escalate to effective war.
Japanese forces ultimately defeated.

1940
13 June President Roosevelt signs a $1.3bn US Navy Bill.

15 June Another US Navy Bill provides for 10,000 new aircraft and 16,000 new air crew for the expanding US Naval air service. Japan has no way of matching this increase.

18 July The 'Two Ocean Navy Expansion Act' is signed by Roosevelt, adding a further 1,325,000 tons of warships and 15,000 more planes to the US Navy.

9 Sep New US government bill for 210 vessels worth $5,500,000,000.

22 Sep Japan 'granted' bases in northern French Indo-China.

27 Sep Japan signs Tripartite Pact with Germany and Italy.

1941
24 July Japanese troops land in southern French Indo-China, beginning occupation on 27 July.

26 Jul US government freezes Japanese assets in the USA and applies a further embargo which will reduce trade by up to 75%. Britain and the Netherlands do likewise.

1 Aug US government places embargoes on aviation fuel and crude oil exports to Japan.

3 Aug Japanese government protests to US over aviation fuel embargo.

Yorktown listing heavily to port, with the destroyer USS *Hammann* standing by.

12 Aug Churchill and Roosevelt sign the Atlantic Charter on board HMS *Prince of Wales*.

26 Nov Japanese attack force, including six aircraft carriers leave Hippotaku Bay for passage to Hawaii.

7 Dec Japan launches attacks on Malaya, Pearl Harbor and the Philippines. The US Pacific Fleet is neutralised, forcing the USN to adopt the carrier and submarine as its new capital vessels.

10 Dec British battleship *Prince of Wales* and battlecruiser *Repulse* are sunk by Indo-China-based Mitsubishi G3M 'Nell' and G4M 'Betty' naval bombers.

11 Dec First Japanese attack on Wake Island fails.

17 Dec Admiral Kimmel, C-in-C US Pacific Fleet, is dismissed.

23–24 Dec Japanese take Wake Island.

25 Dec Hong Kong falls to the Japanese.

31 Dec Nimitz becomes C-in-C US Pacific Fleet.

1942

11 Jan USS *Saratoga* is torpedoed south-west of Hawaii by IJN submarine *I-6*.

Jan Combined Fleet Chief of Staff, Ugaki, includes Midway in future operations draft.

1 Feb US carriers raid Japanese-held Pacific islands.

15 Feb Singapore surrenders.

19 Feb Nagumo's carriers raid Darwin in Northern Australia.

20 Feb Army rejects IJN plan to invade Ceylon. IJN feel they can only move eastward, against the USN.

27 Feb Battle of the Java Sea. The ABDA (American, British, Dutch and Australian) fleet is virtually destroyed by Japanese surface ships.

Feb. Admiral Somerville's Eastern Fleet begins to arrive in Indian Ocean.

1 March Remaining Allied naval forces in the South China Sea are destroyed.

9 March Dutch East Indies fall.

28 March IJN Naval General Staff reluctantly approves the Midway operation in principle. The Combined Fleet Staff now begin detailed work on Operation 'MI'.

2–5 April Kiroshima, Watanabe and the Naval General Staff discuss Midway. Following Yamamoto's threats of resignation, all reluctantly agree to the plan.

2 April Nagumo and his carriers mount a large-scale incursion into the Indian Ocean, attacking shipping and raiding India and Ceylon.

5 April HM Ships *Dorsetshire* and *Cornwall* are sunk by Nagumo's carrier aircraft.

9 April HMS *Hermes* is sunk by Nagumo's carrier aircraft. This is the first carrier to be sunk by shipborne aircraft.

18 April Doolittle Raid on Tokyo, Yokohama, Nagoya, Kobe and Osaka in the Japanese home islands. No significant physical damage.

22 April Admiral Nagumo returns to Japan with his First Air Fleet. He is informed of the Midway operation.

1–4 May Initial 'MI' wargames take place on board the battleship *Yamato*.

3–8 May Battle of the Coral Sea. USS *Lexington* sunk and *Yorktown* badly damaged; the Japanese lose the small carrier *Shoho*, and *Shokaku*'s and *Zuikaku*'s air groups are ravaged. 80% of the Japanese carrier aircraft in this operation are lost, but the IJN believe *Yorktown* sunk.

5 May Naval Order 18 is issued by Admiral Nagumo, authorising Operations 'AL' and 'MI'.

British forces undertake Operation 'Ironclad', the invasion of Madagascar in an attempt to deny the western Indian Ocean to the IJN.

10 May False despatches from Midway concerning water problems are sent on the orders of 'Hypo'.

21 May Midway initiates alert status.

22–26 May Ground and air reinforcements arrive on Midway.

25 May 'Hypo' deciphers timing for attacks on Aleutians and Midway.

26–28 May Japanese Combined Fleet sails from Ominato, Hashirajima, Saipan and Guam for the Midway Operation.

28 May Admiral Spruance and Task Force 16 leave Hawaii for 'Point Luck'.

30 May Admiral Fletcher and Task Force 17 leave Hawaii for 'Point Luck'. Two days late the Japanese submarine 'cordon' arrives on station, thereby failing to detect the passage of the US task forces.

1 June Japan becomes aware of

The sinking destroyer USS *Hammann* after being torpedoed by Japanese submarine, *I-168*. The same submarine also gave the coup de grâce to *Yorktown*.

increased US activity on and near Midway. No action is taken by Yamamoto.

2 June Task Forces 16 and 17 meet at 'Point Luck'.

The Battle of Midway

Note: Times quoted are those traditionally used.

3 June Admiral Tanaka's Midway Invasion Force is discovered by US reconnaissance aircraft. Midway B-17s unsuccessfully bomb this force. Admiral Kakuta's Aleutian Striking Force attacks Dutch Harbor. Little damage is done. More raids follow the next day.

From radio intercepts Yamamoto, but not Nagumo, is informed of possible US task force in vicinity of Midway.

4 June Dawn (?) Admiral Nagumo launches first air strike against Midway from his Midway Striking Force. Second wave held in reserve. US and Japanese fleets begin launching reconnaissance planes.

0430 Japanese carriers launch patrols, followed by Midway strike force. *Akagi, Kaga, Chikuma* and *Haruna* launch search aircraft 1, 2, 5 and 7.

0438 Japanese cruiser *Chikuma* launches search plane 6.

0442 Japanese cruiser *Tone* launches search plane 3.

0500 *Tone* launches final search plane, number 4, over 30 minutes late.

0530 PBYs from Midway sight Japanese Striking Force.

0553 Midway radar detects attacking Japanese aircraft.

0600 Midway Air Garrison readies strike and fighter aircraft.

0603 Spruance (TF.16) receives news of Japanese carriers.

0607 Fletcher (TF.17) orders Spruance (TF.16) to attack Japanese striking force.

0610–0615 Midway Vindicators and Avengers are launched.

0630–0700 Nagumo's carrier aircraft attack Midway

0700 Japanese attack leader requests second Midway strike. Nagumo hesitates. Spruance (TF.16) launches strike against Japanese carriers, completing launch by 0805.

0705–0715 Midway's Avengers unsuccessfully attack *Hiryu*. Marauders from Midway unsuccessfully attack *Akagi*. The US attacks are not co-ordinated.

0715 Nagumo orders second Midway strike. His second-wave aircraft are rearmed with high-explosive anti-land weapons in place of anti-ship weapons.

0728 *Tone*'s search plane 4 sights US ships.

0745 Nagumo asks for clarification of sighting and orders rearming halted.

0800–0820 Nagumo attacked by Midway aircraft, then again unsuccessfully by SBDs, followed by B-17s. Again, attacks are not co-ordinated.

0820 *Tone*'s search plane 4 reports a US carrier.

0830 Japanese Midway strike force returns to IJN carriers. Nagumo begins to recover aircraft before launching his second strike against US ships.

0840 *Yorktown* launches strike aircraft.

0920–0928 *Hornet*'s TBD Devastators

(VT-8) attack Nagumo. No hits scored and all 15 planes are shot down.

0930 *Enterprise*'s TBD Devastators (VT-6) attack Nagumo. No hits are scored and 10 out of 14 planes are shot down.

1000 *Yorktown*'s air group sights Japanese carriers.

1015 *Yorktown*'s TBDs (VT-3) attack Nagumo. No hits are scored and 10 of 12 planes are shot down. Wildcats of VF-3 engage Zero CAP.

1022–1027 *Yorktown*'s SBD Dauntlesses from VB-3 attack, hit and disable *Soryu*. *Enterprise*'s SBDs from VS-6 and VB-6 attack and disable *Akagi* and *Kaga*.

1050 Nagumo transfers his flag from *Akagi* to the cruiser *Nagara* and signals to Yamamoto in the Main Force that three of his carriers have been lost. *Hiryu* launches attack on US fleet.

1220 Yamamoto orders the Midway forces to be concentrated.

1230 *Yorktown* is successfully dive-bombed by *Hiryu*'s D3A 'Vals' and is stopped in the water.

1245 *Hiryu* launches a second strike against the US fleet.

1310 Yamamoto orders suspension of Midway and Aleutians occupation.

1330 Fletcher transfers flag from *Yorktown* to the cruiser *Astoria*.

1400 US submarine *Nautilus* torpedoes *Akagi*.

1440–1442 *Yorktown* is hit again by torpedoes from *Hiryu*'s second-strike aircraft.

1445 A *Yorktown* scout from VS-5 locates Nagumo's last carrier, *Hiryu*.

1500 Crewmen aboard *Yorktown* are ordered to abandon ship.

1530 Spruance launches attack on *Hiryu*.

1700 *Hiryu* is hit and disabled by SBDs from VS-6, VB-6 and VB-3.

1730 Yamamoto reinstates the Aleutians operation.

1913 *Soryu* sinks.

1915 Yamamoto orders a general advance.

1925 *Kaga* sinks.

2255 Yamamoto replaces Nagumo with Kondo, C-in-C 2nd Fleet, to command Midway operation.

5 June

0215 US submarine *Tambor* causes collision between Japanese cruisers *Mogami* and *Mikuma*.

0255 Yamamoto cancels Midway invasion

0455 *Akagi* is sunk by Japanese torpedoes.

0500 *Hiryu* is torpedoed by Japanese destroyer *Makigumo*.

0810–0850 Remaining airworthy *Enterprise*, *Hornet* and Midway Dauntless, Vindicator and B-17 aircraft attack withdrawing Japanese ships, particularly the collision-damaged cruisers.

0900 *Hiryu* sinks.

p.m. Yamamoto orders the Northern Aleutians force to be reinforced.

6 June

1230 Further strikes against the Japanese cruisers. *Mikuma* sinks.

13:30 *Yorktown* is torpedoed, along with *Hammann*, her escorting destroyer, by the Japanese submarine *I-168*. *Hammann* sinks.

7 June 06:00 *Yorktown* finally sinks.

11 June Tokyo press announces a great Japanese naval victory at Midway.

12 June Japanese forces land on Attu Island in the Aleutians. They later occupy Kiska and Attu islands. For more than a year both the Japanese and Americans trade air attacks on each other's land positions, and skirmishes occur. Air attacks by the Americans grow in number until, in August 1943, they successfully regain control of the Aleutians.

Aftermath

7 Aug Guadalcanal and Solomon Islands invaded by US forces (first major US offensive in the Pacific).

1943

March Last naval battle off the Aleutians.

18 April Admiral Isoroku Yamamoto's aircraft is ambushed in mid-air by US P-38 fighters following further successful US code-breaking. He is killed in the ambush.

11 May US forces land on Attu. By 1 June all Japanese resistance has ended.

30 June Commencement of Allied amphibious operations against Japanese-held islands in the south-west Pacific (Operation 'Cartwheel').

US 'island-hopping' campaign thus begins.

15 Aug US forces land on Kiska. No resistance is encountered as Japanese forces have already withdrawn.

1944

18–20 June Battle of the Philippine Sea (or 'Marianas Turkey Shoot'). IJN loses three aircraft carriers and hundreds of aircraft, and Japanese carrier air strength is thereby effectively destroyed.

23–26 Oct Battle of Leyte Gulf. IJN loses four aircraft carriers and three battleships and now seems to be a broken force.

27 Oct First *kamikaze* attacks on US ships (off the Philippines).

1945

18 March First US Navy attacks on Japanese home islands.

1 April US invasion of Okinawa.

6 Aug Hiroshima attacked with atomic weapons.

9 Aug Nagasaki similarly attacked

14–15 Aug Emperor Hirohito broadcasts Japanese surrender statement.

2 Sep Signing of peace treaty on board American battleship *Missouri* in Tokyo Bay.

GLOSSARY

It must be remembered that the Allied reporting name system for Japanese aircraft came into existence following the Battle of Midway. Additionally, a number of US aircraft names only became official after Midway, such as Avenger (Grumman TBM/TBF).

The IJN and the USN employed a similar official coding system for their naval aircraft. For example, the Japanese A6M Zero's designation is explained thus – A = naval fighter, 6 = the sixth type of naval fighter, M = Mitsubishi (the manufacturer of the aircraft). The floatplane version of the Zero, the A6M2-N received this designation as the extra 2 denoted the model of Zero (modified wing and engine etc.), whilst the N stood for Nakajima, who was the manufacturer of the floatplane version. For a much fuller insight into the Japanese coding system see Rene J. Francillon, *Japanese Aircraft of the Pacific War* (London: Putnam & Co, 1970).

The USN used a similar system. For example, in SBD (i.e., Douglas Dauntless), S = scout, B = bomber and D = Douglas, the manufacturer, whilst in F4F (Grumman Wildcat), F = fighter, 4 = fourth such aircraft built by Grumman for the USN and F = Grumman, the manufacturer. Further information in this topic can be obtained from Gordon Swanborough et al., *United States Naval Aircraft Since 1911* (London: Putnam & Co, 1990).

A6M Mitsubishi Reisen or Zero-sen. Japanese carrier-borne interceptor fighter. Known to the Allies as 'Zero', 'Zeke' or 'Hamp'. Still in production at the end of the war. Early in the war *all* Japanese aircraft were being called 'Zero' by the Allies, adding to the myth surrounding the aircraft.

A6M2-N Nakajima floatplane version of the Zero. Employed by Japanese seaplane carriers during Midway. Known to the Allies as 'Rufe'.

AAW Anti-Air Warfare.

'AL' Japanese code-name for the Aleutians diversion during the Midway operation, although 'AL' was actually only the strike against the US forces at Dutch Harbor on Unalaska Island.

'AOB' Japanese code-name for the seizure of Kiska during the Aleutians campaign.

'AQ' Japanese code-name for the seizure of Attu during the Aleutians campaign.

ASW Anti-Submarine Warfare

B-17 USAAF Boeing Flying Fortress long-range, land based, four-engine medium bomber.

B-26 USAAF Martin Marauder land-based twin-engine light bomber.

B5N Nakajima-built, three-seat carrier torpedo- and level-bomber, known to the Allies as 'Kate'.

CAP Combat air patrol

Opposite page: Japanese Foreign Minister Namoru Shigemitsu signs the Japanese surrender aboard the battleship USS *Missouri* in Tokyo Bay as high-ranking Allied officers look on, 2 September 1945.

CV Fleet aircraft carrier. Usually a carrier with a displacement in excess of 20,000 tons and an air group of over 50 aircraft (though often nearer 70).

CVL Small/light aircraft carrier. Generally under 20,000 tons and with an air group of around 30 machines.

D3A Aichi-built two-seat, carrier-based bomber, known to the Allies as 'Val'.

E13A Aichi-built, long-range reconnaissance floatplane. Based on Japanese cruisers and battleships during Midway. Known to the Allies as 'Jake'.

F1M Mitsubishi two-seat patrol and reconnaissance floatplane. Employed by Japanese battleships during Midway. Known to the Allies as 'Pete'.

F2A Brewster Buffalo single-seat carrier-borne fighter. The USN's first monoplane carrier fighter to enter service. Relegated to a land-based role and employed by the USMC by the time of the Midway operation.

F4F Grumman Wildcat single-seat USN carrier-borne fighter. (Aircraft built by General Motors were known as FM-1 and FM-2.) Employed by USN carriers and by the USMC from Midway.

IJN Imperial Japanese Navy.

'MI' Japanese code-name for the operation to seize Midway Islands that would lead to the destruction of the US Pacific Fleet.

'MO' Japanese code-name for the strike against, and seizure of, Port Moresby. This led to the Battle of the Coral Sea in May 1942.

PBY Consolidated Catalina, the USN's long-range maritime patrol-bomber flying boat. Based at Midway.

SBD Douglas Dauntless two-seat USN carrier-based scout/dive-bomber. Nicknamed the 'Slow But Deadly' by some.

SB2U Vought Vindicator two-seat, carrier- based scout/dive-bomber. Land-based at Midway and employed by the USMC. Nicknamed 'Wind Indicator' by some of its air crews.

TBD Douglas Devastator three-seat USN carrier-based torpedo bomber.

TBF Grumman Avenger three-seat USN carrier-based torpedo bomber (but they were land-based during the Midway operation. (Aircraft built by General Motors were designated TBM.)

TF Task Force (US).

USAAC United States Army Air Corps.

USAAF United States Army Air Force. The USAAC was redesignated USAAF on 20 June 1941 though many still referred to the service as the USAAC.

USMC United States Marine Corps.

USN United States Navy.

VB US Navy carrier bomber squadron.

VF US Navy carrier fighter squadron.

VMF US Marine Corps fighter squadron.

VMSB US Marine scout-bomber squadron.

VS US Navy scout-bomber squadron.

VT US Navy torpedo-bomber squadron.

BIBLIOGRAPHY

The following is a list – far from comprehensive – of titles that either have Midway at their heart or have substantial elements contained within them dealing with the Midway operation. It should be noted that works written before 1978 did not have full access to, or complete knowledge of, the importance of the intelligence sources and their implications. From that year, the US government began to declassify these sources.

Agawa, H. *The Reluctant Admiral* (Kodansha International, 1979)

Argyle, C. J. *Japan at War: 1937–1945* (London: Arthur Baker, 1976)

Ballard, R. D., and Archbold, R. *Return to Midway* (London: Cassell & Co., 1999)

Barker, A. J. *Midway: The Turning Point* (London: Macdonald & Co, 1971)

Bateson, C. *The War with Japan* (New York: 1968)

Beach, E. L. *The United States Navy* (New York: Henry Holt & Co., 1986)

Bicheno, H. *Midway* (London: Cassell & Co., 2001)

Bryan, J., 'The Battle of Midway', in Congdon, D. *Combat: Pacific Theater – World War II* (New York: Dell Publishing Co., 1958)

Chesneau, R. *Aircraft Carriers of the World, 1914 to the Present: An Illustrated Encyclopedia* (London: Arms and Armour Press, 1984)

Costello, J. *The Pacific War, 1941–45* (London: 1989)

Cowley, R., (ed.) *What If? Military Historians Imagine What Might Have Been* (London: Macmillan, 2000)

Creed, R. *PBY: The Catalina Flying Boat* (Shrewsbury: Airlife, 1986)

Cressman, R. J. 'Blaze of Glory: Charlie Ware and the Battle of Midway', in *The Hook*, 24, No 1, Spring 1996

Cressman, R. J. 'Flight to Midway', *Marine Corps Gazette*, 65, No 5, May 1981

Drea, E. J. *MacArthur's ULTRA: Codebreaking and the War Against Japan: 1942–45* (Lawrence: 1992)

Dull, P. S. *A Battle History of the Imperial Japanese Navy* (Annapolis: US Naval Institute Press, 1978)

Ellis, J. *Brute Force: Allied Strategy and Tactics in the Second World War* (London: Andre Deutsch, 1990)

Francillon, R. *Japanese Aircraft of the Pacific War* (London: Putnam, 1987)

Friedman, N. *Carrier Air Power* (Annapolis: United States Naval Institute Press, 1981)

Fuchida, M., and Masatake, O. *Midway: The Battle that Doomed Japan* (Annapolis: 1955)

Fuller, R., *Shokan: Hirohito's Samurai – Leaders of the Japanese Armed Forces, 1926–1945* (London: Arms & Armour Press, 1992)

Goodspeed, H. 'Always Faithful', *Naval Aviation*, Vol. 85, No 4, May–June 2003

Goldstein, D. M., and Dillon, K. V. *The Pearl Harbor Papers: Inside the Japanese Plans* (Dulles: Brassey's, 2000)

Grenfell, R. *Main Fleet to Singapore* (London: Faber and Faber, 1951)

Hamer, D. *Bombers versus Battleships* (London: Conway Maritime Press, 1999)

Hashimoto, M. *Sunk: The Story of the Japanese Submarine Fleet, 1942–1945* (London: Cassell & Co.)

Hargis, R. *US Naval Aviator: 1941–45* (London: Osprey, 2002)

Hata, I., and Izawa, Y. *Japanese Naval Aces and Fighter Units in World War II* (Shrewsbury: Airlife, 1989)

Healy, M. *The Battle of Midway* (London: Osprey, 1993)

Horikoshi, J. *Eagles of Mitsubishi: The Story of the Zero Fighter* (London: Orbis Publishing, 1982)

Horner, D. *The Second World War: The Pacific* (London: Osprey, 2002)

Howorth, S., (ed.) *Men of War: Great Naval Leaders of World War II* (London: Weidenfeld & Nicolson, 1992)

Howorth, S. *Morning Glory: A History of the Imperial Japanese Navy* (London: Hamish Hamilton, 1983)

Humble, R. *Naval Warfare: An Illustrated History* (London: Orbis Publishing, 1983)

Ienaga, S. *The Pacific War: World War II and the Japanese, 1931–1945* (New York: 1978)

Ito, M., and Pineau, R. *The End of the Imperial Japanese Navy* (Exeter: Wheaton & Co., 1962)

Layton, E. T. *And I Was There: Pearl Harbor and Midway – Breaking the Secrets* (NY: 1985)

Levite, A. *Intelligence and Surprise* (New York: Columbia University Press, 1987)

Lewin, R. *The Other Ultra: Codes, Ciphers and the Defeat of Japan* (London: 1982)

Lord, W. *Midway: The Incredible Victory* (USA: Harper & Row, 1967)

Mikesh, R. C., and Abe, S. *Japanese Aircraft, 1910–1941* (London: Putnam & Co., 1993)

— *Japanese Aircraft: Code Names and Designations* (Pennsylvania: Schiffer Publishing, 1993)

Morison, S. E. *The Two Ocean War* (New England: Little, Brown & Co., 1963)

Okumiya, M., Horikoshi, J., and Caidin, M. *Zero: The Story of the Japanese Navy Air Force, 1937–1945* (London: Corgi, 1958)

Parshall, J. B., Dickson, D. D., and Tully, A. P. 'Doctrine Matters: Why the Japanese Lost at Midway', *Naval War College Review*, Summer 2001

Peattie, M. R. *Sunburst: The Rise of Japanese Naval Air Power, 1909–1941* (Annapolis: Naval Institute Press, 2001)

Peattie, M. R., et al, *Kaigun* (Annapolis: Naval Institute Press, 1997)

Potter, E. B. *Nimitz* (Annapolis: Naval Institute Press, 1976)

Potter, J. D. *Yamamoto: The Man Who Menaced America* (New York: Viking Press, 1965)

Prange, G. W. *Miracle at Midway* (New York: 1982)

Prange, G. W., Goldstein, D. M., and Dillion, K. V. *God's Samurai* (USA: Brassey's, 1990)

Reynolds, C. G. *War in the Pacific* (New York: 1990)

Robbins, G. *The Aircraft Carrier Story: 1908–1945* (London: Cassell & Co., 2001)

Rubel, R. C. 'Gettysburg and Midway: Historical Parallels in Operational Command', *Naval War College Review*, Winter 1995

Smith, P. C. *Douglas SBD Dauntless* (Marlborough: The Crowood Press, 1997)

— *The Battle of Midway* (London: New English Library, 1976)

Spector, R. H. *The Eagle Against the Sun: The American War with Japan* (NY: 1985)

Swanborough, G., and Bowers, P. M. *United States Navy Aircraft Since 1911* (London: Putnam & Co., 1990)

Sweetman, J., (ed.) *The Great Admirals: Command at Sea, 1587–1945* (Annapolis: Naval Institute Press, 1997)

Symonds, C. L. *The Naval Institute Historical Atlas of the US Navy* (Annapolis: Naval Institute Press, 1995)

Tagaya, O. *Imperial Japanese Naval Aviator: 1937–45* (London: Osprey, 2002)

Thomas, D. *Japan's War at Sea* (London: 1978)

Thomas, G. *US Navy Carrier Aircraft Colours: Units, Colours, Markings and Operations during World War 2* (Surrey: Air Research Publications, 1989)

Trotti, J. *Marine Air: First to Fight* (California: Presidio Press, 1985)

Tuleja, T. V. *Climax At Midway* (London: J. M. Dent & Sons, 1960)

Ugaki, M. *Fading Victory: The Diary of Admiral Matome Ugaki* (Pittsburgh: University of Pittsburgh Press, 1991)

Van der Vat, D. *The Pacific Campaign* (London: Grafton, 1992)

Whitley, M. J. *Cruisers of World War Two: An International Encyclopedia* (London: Arms and Armour Press, 1995)

Wildenberg, T. *Destined for Glory: Dive Bombing, Midway, and the Evolution of Carrier Airpower* (Annapolis: Naval Institute Press, 1998)

Wilmott, H. P. *The Banner and the Javelin: Japanese and Allied Strategies, February to June 1942* (Annapolis: 1983)

Winnefeld, J. A., and Johnson, D. J. *Joint Air Operations: Pursuit of Unity in Command and Control, 1942–1991* (USA: RAND, 1993)

Winton, J. *Air Power at Sea, 1939–45* (London: Sidgwick & Jackson, 1976)

Woodbury Isom, D. 'The Battle of Midway: Why the Japanese Lost', *Naval War College Review*, Summer 2000

INDEX